The Hour of the Wolf

a memoir

Fatima Bhutto

Scribner

New York   Amsterdam/Antwerp   London
Toronto   Sydney/Melbourne   New Delhi

Scribner

An Imprint of Simon & Schuster, LLC

1230 Avenue of the Americas

New York, NY 10020

This is a work of nonfiction. Some identifying details have been changed.

First Scribner hardcover edition January 2026

SCRIBNER and design are trademarks of Simon & Schuster, LLC

For information about special discounts for bulk purchases, please contact Simon & Schuster Special Sales at 1-866-506-1949 or business@simonandschuster.com.

The Simon & Schuster Speakers Bureau can bring authors to your live event. For more information or to book an event, contact the Simon & Schuster Speakers Bureau at 1-866-248-3049 or visit our website at www.simonspeakers.com.

Interior design by Kyle Kabel

Manufactured in the United States of America

1   3   5   7   9   10   8   6   4   2

Library of Congress Control Number: 2025937610

ISBN 978-1-6680-7562-3
ISBN 978-1-6682-3003-9 (Int/Can Exp)
ISBN 978-1-6680-7564-7 (ebook)

Portions of this book were previously published in *Granta* 158 in 2022.

For Mir and Caspian
and for Graham, who gave me everything

Something eerie ties us to the world of animals. Sometimes the animals pull you backward into it. You share hunger and fear with them like salt in blood.

—Barry Lopez, *Arctic Dreams*

The Hour of the Wolf

Chapter 1

One day I see a wild deer. It is evening, the second month of lockdown in the spring of the pandemic. I am outside in my friend MC's garden with my pregnant dog, Coco. She is days away from delivery, her very first, but she doesn't look like she is pregnant at all: her stomach is almost concave, and aside from a week when she was ravenous, her appetite is delicate, her mood strange. The vets in this Oxfordshire village where my best friend, Allegra, and I have decamped to ride out what we imagine will be the only wave of this virus won't give us an appointment. "It's not an emergency," they tell me on the phone, "we are only seeing emergencies during Covid." No one knows what Covid is yet, none of us knows how to behave. What does the virus have to do with a pregnant dog?

My dog's stomach is hollow, there is stillness when I place my hand on her belly. It's not a phantom pregnancy, she's had one of those before. We had a scan, and it confirmed that she is carrying a litter of puppies. But something doesn't feel right. "She sounds fine," these new vets—who we don't know and have never met—tell me on the phone. We are not from Oxford—we are far from home.

Beyond the lockdown and this new terrain, I am in further limbo because I have spent nearly a decade waiting for a man who has made promise after promise to me and, diligently and with impressive commitment, has broken them all. We are both unmarried. He confesses that he has never met a woman he could settle down with until me, that I am the first woman he has wanted to build a life with. But I come from a public family and have chosen to be a writer, hardly the life of a private civilian. He has his reasons. The man tells me that this public gaze makes him uncomfortable, maybe things will change in the future but for now he wants nothing to do with it. I can't change who I am, but neither can he. He would like it very much if I didn't drag him and our relationship out into the open, where he believes it will lose everything that is special about it. And it is special. I am hypnotized by him. He is unlike anyone that I have ever met: uninhibited, blazingly sure of himself, so much so that he calls his parents "darling" when he speaks to them, as though he is the parent. It also doesn't hurt that he is beautiful, rugged, and old-school masculine. He tells me that we are soul mates. And so I don't resist the hidden quality he demands of our relationship. I just want to be with him. I will do anything. Tell people about us? Why tempt people's envy? Meet my friends? No, he'd rather not, thanks. Meet his? Why? What do you need to meet them for? Live together? Get engaged? Oh no, that's not how things are done. These things take time. Besides, he's not sure he's cut out for that sort of life. He's a free spirit. Marry? Please.

But there is so much that is precious about what we have, he reminds me when I despair at the dictates he has laid down, how can I not see that? He persuades me to follow him, to believe in him. I am thirty-eight years old and have no family, no children, no one besides a small Jack Russell as my charge. It feels uncomfortable to say that this man isolated me from my world, but, in effect, I've since realized, he did.

The man is older than I am, and initially I believe that he knows so much more about life than I do; after all, he knows how to face all manner of difficulties with calm and sangfroid and always seems to get his way. He expended no effort on how he dressed or looked, wearing the same shirt three days in a row, but was somehow always radiant with a large smile and warm, tanned face and green eyes that crinkled at the corners when he laughed. If he woke up one morning and decided that he wanted to learn how to parachute, he'd just go off and learn, flinging himself off a cliff or out of an airplane as though it were the most natural thing in the world. As a result, there was seemingly nothing that he didn't know how to do—skiing, motorcycle riding, martial arts, tennis, photography, baking. You name it, the man did it. Nothing made him nervous; on the contrary, he seemed to delight in things that would give the rest of us pause—walking through rough neighborhoods late at night, getting lost in unknown places, changing plans and disrupting itineraries midway through travel. He was a terrible dancer, but who cared? He was so confident, if he felt like it, he danced anyway.

The established confines that restricted the rest of us from behaving like libertines didn't apply to him. He was a teetotaler who never smoked, but still a pleasure seeker. If he wanted to spend a day in a botanical garden, examining the roots of rare plants, he just did that—no matter what else you might have had planned. If a shop he felt like visiting was closing, he persuaded the owners to keep the shutters up just a bit longer, and before they knew it, they'd changed their opening hours, only for him to mosey around for as long as he liked and leave without buying a thing.

He seemed to have no fear, no shame, no embarrassment, and no respect for other people's boundaries, even though he guarded his own fiercely. He could tell you what kind of person a total stranger was by observing them for five minutes—proving himself correct by going up to said stranger afterward and asking them to confirm his private hypotheses—and when he was in the mood, he could be a great mimic and funny, and he was a patient and generous teacher. When he wanted to help you, he would devote hours and days to your problems.

When he turned his bright attention to you, you felt as though you had been baptized into some intimate and glorious order. The man had an extraordinary ability to make you feel that he alone understood you and had some unique insight into what ailed you. When I saw his attention drift, when he turned toward someone else who had a problem that needed solving, like a teacher's pet, I became jealous. I wanted his attention, all of it. When he sensed this, he did the opposite of reassuring me: he would cut me off, depriving me of exactly what I wanted. My mood became quickly tethered to his; I needed him to feel safe, secure, to feel good. He was demanding and difficult from the outset, and though he could be dazzling, handsome, and intelligent, he also had an indefatigable capacity to be cruel.

Understanding this dynamic, and how much I needed him, he seemed to take a certain delight in putting me down, in disparaging my country or finding positive reviews of my work and asking me, with incredulity, if I really believed any of that praise. I never showed him my writing because no matter what a piece was about, he was always a breath away from telling me that my thinking was facile, or that I was trying too hard to prove I was clever (there was never a bad occasion to remind me that he was smarter than I was), or that I didn't understand the issue I had written about, not deeply, not like he did.

He also had fits of rage. Many times, when we were sitting in a restaurant, if I happened to say something he didn't like, he would shout at me, stand up, and storm off. He went through moods that lasted days when he would simply stop talking to me, even if we were out together, as though I no longer existed. He would smile at a waitress and compliment her shoes, or ask her what her name meant and listen with fascination just to show me that he could speak nicely to someone if he wished, he just didn't wish to speak to me. On the occasions when I would tell him I was leaving if he insisted on dragging me around while ignoring me, he would glower at me and threaten me in a low voice: "If you leave, you will never see me again for as long as you live."

As an accompaniment to his cruelty and anger, he had a sense of humor that could be childish and mean. He taunted you with exactly what he knew would hurt, laughing in your face as you tried to recover your composure. One day, out of the blue, he bit my hand so hard that I lost feeling in the area where my thumb meets the flesh of my palm. Nothing had happened to provoke the bite (what possibly could have happened?)—I was looking at my phone and he was playing chess on my iPad when he just reached over and bit me so hard that even after the bite marks had faded and the bruise had gone down, I couldn't move my thumb without discomfort. He thought it was funny. Months later, in London, I went to an acupuncturist I sometimes saw for headaches and showed him my hand, as it was still in pain. He looked at it quietly while I thought of what to say. My brother bit me? But one brother was twenty-five then and the other eleven. I walked into a door with my hand? "I, uh, was playing with my dog," I said sheepishly, "and she bit me." "That badly?" the acupuncturist asked. I didn't have the heart to furnish the lie. "Actually, I think it's a damaged nerve from a previous injury."

My dog would never, ever bite me.

I was always able to excuse the man for some reason or another: he works hard, he has a complex character, he had a painful childhood, he's stressed, he's not used to expressing himself. These were all excuses he had fed me about his behavior, sighing resignedly as he admitted these seemingly unfixable faults. I forgave him over and over because I loved him. And I knew, no matter how he acted, that he loved me too. And admittedly, there was something in me that found our strange, disjointed situation convenient, romantic even, fueled by spontaneity and impulse rather than dreary domestic routine. I am independent and need plenty of room to myself in order not to feel suffocated. In the early years, I didn't mind that we lived in different cities. It suited me. I sensed the man was controlling and I didn't want to be controlled. I was happy having my own life, I had friends and work I loved, and there in my life, the life that was lived apart from the man, there was no one keeping me under surveillance and passing judgment on everything I did.

When he visited me, I simply dropped out of my own life and shifted everything around in order to focus all my attention on him. I enjoyed our time together and imagined that this split double life was not only manageable but exciting. Sometimes we would meet every month, other times every three months.

Of course, this life by long distance would end one day, one day soon, if only I could just be patient, the man has sworn. One day, we would be together and have a life, a real life, one where secrets would be banished, roots put down, and promises kept. But after nine years I have grown tired of being patient and have begun to suspect that the man lies far too often, about everything, with profound sincerity if not admiration about his own decency and honor.

Walking in my friend MC's perfumed garden with my dog in the quiet evenings of April 2020, I sometimes wonder if

I can just disappear here, into the Oxfordshire countryside, where the man has never been and will not be able to find me. It seems an attractive possibility. Not least because I still do not have the strength to leave him myself.

Coco sees the doe at the same time as I do. She is large, tall, and noble, her skin reddish in the twilight. My dog is small, less than four pounds with the weight of her nonphantom babies. She descends from hunters and ratters and loves to dive into rabbit warrens, run up trees, burrow and dig and pirouette, and, though she is the gentlest creature I have ever known, thrilled by the chase but never by the kill, she took a rabbit by the throat the other day. MC—who is a garden designer, with a heritage garden in which she grows deep purple irises, plump red roses, and perfumed magnolia trees—was thrilled. The rabbits eat all her precious plants. "Well done, Coco," MC cooed as Coco proudly wagged her curly tail over her prey. I didn't praise her, but I understood. She was hunting to be sure there would be food for her young. Now, Coco glares at the wild deer, her spine arched, the hair on her neck standing on end, and her lithe, balletic body trembling, ready to catch and kill the doe too.

In his book *Of Wolves and Men*, Barry Lopez describes the moment a hunter and its prey lock eyes. A decision is made then, Lopez says, in this moment he calls "the conversation of death." There is ritual in the exchange between hunter and hunted: the hunted surrenders his body and flesh and in exchange, receives the hunter's respect for his sacrifice. One animal must kill to live, to feed the old and the young of his pack, and the other must surrender himself to protect *his* brethren, his old and young, from being taken. There is, Lopez writes in his ethnography of wolves, a dignity in this encounter—both animals, not just the predator, make a choice in this ceremony. They agree on death. "When the wolf 'asks' for the life of another animal he is responding to something in that animal that says, 'My life is strong. It is worth asking for.' The nobility of this death is that it is appropriate, it is a chosen death. Not a tragedy. 'I have lived a full life,' says the prey. 'I am ready to die. I am willing to die because clearly I will be dying so that the others in this small herd will go on living.'"[1]

When I think of the idea of a chosen death, I think of my father, Mir Murtaza. He was a member of parliament in Pakistan and was forty-two years old when he was killed, but he made the decision to give his life long before that, when he was a young man, just after his father was assassinated. My father raised me on his own until I was seven years old. He made our life, lived in exile during the dark days of Pakistan's dictatorship in the 1980s, a game of fun and mystery. He believed the politics that surrounded our family, as well as the deaths and violence, were no reason to live in fear. I may often still have been afraid, suffering stomachaches throughout my childhood that were so debilitating I could barely stand upright until they had passed, but my father taught me to be grateful and to be brave. The world was wondrous and there was curiosity and warmth in all its offerings. Though my father loved his time on earth, he knew that when they came to take his life, he would give them it. There was a beauty to him, a romance to how he saw the world, no matter its cruelties. I think it came from that acceptance, what Nietzsche called *amor fati*, a love of one's fate. It is a radical choice not to "merely bear what is necessary," Nietzsche wrote, "but love it."[2] The brave meet death with courage, as there is no other choice.

My father was killed on his way home from a political meeting on the outskirts of Karachi. All the streetlights on our road had been shut off, and there were a hundred policemen in wait, some high in the trees in sniper positions. When my father, who was a vocal critic of the state's corruption, as well as the extrajudicial killings for which Karachi's police have long been famous, got out of the car, a signal was fired in the air by an officer charged with identifying my father, the single shot an order to commence firing. My father and six of his comrades were killed, all left to bleed to death on the road. I was footsteps away, a teenager waiting for her father to return at the end of the day. The police held us back from coming outside to see what had happened. They never took the men to hospitals with ERs but dropped each of them off at a different clinic around the city, not one capable of saving lives. No matter what people tell me, I know my father suffered and I know he must have been in pain.

My father loved animals. They were drawn to him. If there was an animal in the room, it inevitably gravitated toward him, seeking his comfort and attention. He was gentle, devoting his curiosity to the animals as though in conversation with them. When my childhood dog, a Belgian shepherd called Pedro, bit me because I was annoying him by trying to sit on him, I went howling to my father, who picked me up and let me cry into his perfectly ironed shirt. "Hit him," I demanded, between tears, "he hurt me." My father was quiet, ignoring me. When I asked him again to reprimand the dog, he said no. "I won't hit him. You were at fault. Don't be rough with Pedro."

Though my father hunted as a young man, going out for *shikar* with his father and brother in rural Larkana, stalking wild boar, I have no memories of him hunting as an adult. He took my brother Zulfikar fishing but more as a ploy for the two of them to spend nights out on a rickety boat, eating under the stars and singing songs from *The Jungle Book*. Before my father's murder I thought animals were animals and humans were humans and a gulf separated the enormity between our feelings and experiences. Though

I had grown up with the ever-present threat of violence and the understanding that it could come for those I loved at any time, with no warning, as I grew older I started to notice that same threat hovering sharply between humans and animals. We have a horrendous ability to inflict cruelty upon animals at will, without repercussion. You see this on the streets, in the way stray animals shrink from the sight of our shadows. My brother felt this instinctively and deeply, long before I did. He couldn't bear scenes of violence toward animals, not in cartoons or in films, where the violence is presented as comic and casual, or in real life, whether it was the goats lining the streets of Karachi before Eid ul Azha, bleating helplessly, ready for slaughter, or a bird that flew into our window, momentarily stunned from the impact. I notice it all the time now, not just how much animals endure: but how noble they are in surrender, how much dignity they possess in the face of a ceaselessly violent world.

To many of us, there is nothing on earth greater or grander or more sophisticated than the self, than ourselves. This is our great failure as a species. We use all our strengths, intelligence, and time in pursuit of the shallow belief that we are special. It is an ancient idea, constantly at war with that essential truth spoken thousands of years ago by Buddha: there is no self. We are not unique, and no essence of ours will remain. Ultimately, we, like everything else on earth, are pure matter, dust. It is how we are born and how we will end, absorbed into the earth and forgotten.

Coco is no wolf, no savior, no prince among men. She is a Jack Russell terrier, the size and hysteria of a mongoose, at best. She has no chance against a deer. But she doesn't know that. She is lit by a primal confidence, a natural stalker enlivened by the scent of a beautiful adversary. MC tells me later that the deer, who also devour her plants, are Muntjacs, and that they have come to Oxfordshire from China, introduced in the early twentieth century. But escapes and deliberate releases of Muntjacs into the wild have resulted in feral populations loose across the United Kingdom. I learn later that Muntjacs are known as barking deer because of their unique cries. I think of their impossible journey from Asia to this soggy island for days afterward. What small imaginations we have, shocked and stupefied at how particles and viruses can travel the breadth of the earth while hungry deer make slow processions around the globe under our very noses.

Back in MC's verdant garden, Coco holds the doe's gaze for five seconds and then, conversation exchanged, leaps at it, heart pounding, racing, running to be joined in ceremony. But the deer escapes. It doesn't jump over the garden fence, it doesn't hit the brick and mortar of the home, it just disappears, vanishes. We never see it again.

Chapter 2

Coco has been with me since she was three months old. I adopted her in 2015 as a gift for my youngest brother, Mir Ali. He had asked for a girl dog, named her after a Japanese cartoon character, even decided where she would sleep—with him, at the foot of his bed. In the two nights that it took to vaccinate her and fly her from London to Pakistan, I fell in love with her and, by the time we reached Karachi, I was already wondering how best to break the bad news to a ten-year-old boy. But on meeting my brother, Coco immediately growled at him, snarling, showing off her sharp little teeth. "The good news is I got a dog," I told Mir Ali warmly. "The bad news is that she's mine."

Mir Ali seemed disappointed, but there was no escaping the fact that every time he tried to touch her, she bared her fangs at him. It turned out for the best. As a matter of principle, Coco hates children. She isn't fond of other people or dogs either. As a pup she barked at strangers on the road, incensed that others might walk on the very street she was using. When she doesn't like someone (this is often), she has been known to yap tirelessly at them until they go away. She is exceedingly bright and loving to a select few, but she is, to put it mildly, a character. Though I have had dogs all my life, Coco is my first real companion. I cared for her and she for me at a point when I was figuring out how to live, how to remake a world of my own, alone.

In those lonely years being with and waiting for the man, Coco and I traveled continents and finally set up a quiet life together. Only she knew the full truth about "the situation," as the man clinically called it. Many arguments about his ruptured promises on "moving forward" (getting married) or "that again" (me wanting to have a child) or "here we go" (my unhappiness at this bizarre, unfulfilling, clandestine life) were swiftly ended by him getting angry and accusing me of not caring for "*his* situation" (more important by far than "*the* situation") before storming out, leaving me alone in whatever restaurant we had been eating in or park we were walking through. Attempts to solve his "situation" were simply "my agenda."

As anxious as I was, as uncertain of how to carve out a small corner for myself, over the years I somehow managed to care for Coco, and not only did she survive but she grew, she learned, adapted, and even thrived. A model writer's dog, she sits quietly for hours while I work, holding a ball between her paws, her body tensed but patient. When her store of patience finally runs out, she jumps up to my lap and rests her warm throat in the crook of my elbow so I cannot write or type. Always cautious, Coco turns to look at me in the park when she spots a pigeon—*shall we chase him?*—awaiting approval and confirmation that this is something I'd like her to do on our behalf. My friends often tease me for how much I speak to Coco. The times I have been angry with her have been when she has run across traffic in chase of a cat without checking with me first, overturned the garbage, jumped on the kitchen table to eat all the food, or kicked off her nappy when she's in heat to smear blood all over the floor in decorative trails. I get angry because I know I cannot protect her in her world, the animal world, but these moments remind me I cannot protect her in mine either.

At night, my dog burrows like the terrier she is, under the covers of my bed. Only once she has rooted and rustled, sleeping for a while in the den-like dark under the blankets, does she slowly drift up until she is on the pillow and we are nose to nose. When I hold her and stroke her, telling her how clever she is, how pretty, how good, she closes her eyes and sighs, breathing softly.

Perhaps one of the man's best qualities was that he loved dogs. As withholding as he could be with me, he was normally warm and loving with Coco. He cooed to her in a voice he never used any other time, gentle and undemanding. He delighted in playing with her, and he pleaded with me, time and again, to let Coco have puppies so he could have a little Coco of his own. Finally, he persuaded me. I wanted her to have a litter because it was essential for her health and general life experience. It wasn't because I wanted children, was desperate for my own, and felt I could do nothing about it. It would be good for her, becoming a mother, good for me too, good for us, I said to myself.

Twenty-five miles from Kathmandu is Namo Buddha. The road there is choppy, bumpy, choked with the smog of scooters and trucks and jeeps, some with stickers of Prince Siddhartha, cross-legged and serene, plastered on their rear windows. It is there, at the Namo Buddha Stupa, that Buddha encountered a starving tigress. The tigress, her body hollowed and drooping, was close to death. Already her cubs had no food. When she died, they would too. Overcome with compassion, Buddha gave himself to her, feeding the tigress his body so that she and her cubs could survive.

I traveled to Namo Buddha in 2016, alone, on assignment for a magazine. The tigers are mostly all gone now—there are just over two hundred free from captivity in Nepal. I went to the stupa, a dusty mound, away from the oxblood walls of the Thrangu Tashi Yangtse monastery, where young boys with shaved heads chant prayers. There was no one else there, save for an old lady selling amulets on a rickety table.

It was on that journey to Nepal that I first became enchanted with the wild. In Chitwan, days earlier, I had tracked the vanishing tigers—seen their claw marks on the bark of aged trees, smelled their scent—but never seen them. With a guide, I trekked into the jungle at dawn, at dusk, on foot, in cars. I went bird-watching and bathed a wounded elephant. I had never been so close to the living world before, never so transfixed. I was so lonely; being close to nature comforted me, soothed me.

God is everywhere in the wilderness—in the mist that travels through a forest at dawn, in the dew that nourishes the soil, in the delicate birds and scavengers. If not there, then where is God?

It was in a deer park that Buddha gave his first sermon. And there, among the monks as Buddha expounded the Four Noble Truths—"I teach suffering—its origin, cessation, and path. That is all I teach,"—was a doe, listening.[3]

Chapter 3

Back in Oxfordshire, Coco's due date came and went. Her stomach never grew, she never put on any weight throughout the entire pregnancy, even though she became sluggish and her energy sank to nothing. Dogs, like humans, have morning sickness, throwing up yellow bile and suffering fluctuations in appetite. I clung to the fact that Coco had experienced both these things. A phone call to her usual vet in London raised my alarms: they insisted she should absolutely be checked. The Oxfordshire vets begrudgingly consented, and so, in a mask and gloves, I brought Coco for a checkup.

No humans were allowed into the clinic, Covid protocols were still new and strange, and Coco was taken from the car straining at her leash and refusing to budge. She returned twenty minutes later, leaping, desperate to escape the vet, who told me from a distance that yes, she was fine, he had seen the pups. Two of them, their heads and spines growing nicely. It should be any day now, he reassured me.

When I told other friends who knew something of the world of dogs and had had litters of their own, they went quiet. Only two puppies? they asked, are you sure? I had always felt something wasn't right. But I read the books and prepared the whelping box and bought the vet-bed fleece, and forceps and scales, calcium and glucose, everything that I could possibly need. I wrote out a list of warning signs for the two friends I was with in case the delivery happened while I was out running in the park nearby or working in MC's sitting room, which I had claimed as my office.

I had been staying with Allegra in London when I adopted Coco. I had texted her, having forgotten to mention that I was spending my day getting a dog, to ask would it be okay if I brought a dog home? Just for two nights? Allegra's home is beautiful, furnished with exquisite taste, not a cushion out of place. I joke that she is obsessed by lampshades, but there is no joke there. She is running out of lamps to put them on. Soon, we will have to wear them. Ever generous, Allegra consented. When she came home that evening and saw a little pup dancing on her antique carpet, she smiled and asked me to make sure I washed her paws and my hands every time we returned from the outside. She liked Coco but didn't particularly want her on her bed or sitting on the chairs around the kitchen table because of germs.

Allegra's caution lasted about a day. Today, she and Coco go walking for hours in the park. Allegra mushes up dog food with her fingers and sings Coco good morning songs and buys her treats, hiding them in her room so when they are curled up together on the bed, where Coco sprawls luxuriantly, she can feed her one, two, or three, stroking the patterned crown on Coco's head.

In Oxfordshire, I read the emergency list to Allegra and MC twice, at lunch and dinner, to make sure they remembered the salient points.

- *Pain is normal, dogs tear at their bedding during labor.*
- *Blood should be expected, normal.*
- *Green discharge before any puppies arrive is not normal— a vet should be called immediately; it means something is seriously wrong.*
- *Green discharge after a puppy or in between puppies, however, is fine. Normal.*
- *Anything longer than 20 minutes of consistent pushing could be bad, though each pup could take up to three hours to be delivered.*

Everyone in our little lockdown bubble was prepared.

Coco's labor began on a Monday morning. While she was lazing in her whelping box, snoozing in a sliver of early spring sun, the contractions started and so did she, jumping up and yelping. After she recovered from the shock, she scuttled around the bed in anxious circles, pulling at the blanket with her teeth and shredding it with her paws. I called the vet; they told me to be patient, most births happened in the middle of the night. I confirmed their emergency number. They told me they'd talk to me the next morning, but I confirmed it anyway. The day passed slowly. Coco nibbled at her food and sat in my lap. Hours later, no sign of an impending birth, we went to sleep. I lay on the bed facing her whelping box, listening to her breathe in the dark.

Just after midnight, Coco woke me up crying. She wanted to go outside. Foggily, I put on my boots and turned on the light as we went down the stairs. I clipped on her leash—the books said pregnant dogs burrow under hedges, seeking privacy and quiet when they're ready to deliver—and we ventured out. In the dark, wet garden, Coco ran in little loops with her nose close to the earth, sniffing for something until she found a spot to relieve herself.

Back inside, Coco trotted back up the stairs. I was still woozy with sleep when we entered the bedroom and I saw the marks on the carpet, small curlicues of wispy stains. I bent down and looked, blinking to make sure. They were green.

I am not a naturalist, not a biologist, not an environ-mentalist. I don't know anything scientific about animals except that I care for them and grew up around them. There are raging debates about whether we should or should not anthropomorphize animals. Frans de Waal, the famous primatologist, dismisses the strange, distancing language that's commonly used among people who study animals. For those zoologists, a kiss is not a kiss but "mouth-to-mouth contact," animals that have fought and made up don't reconcile but engage in "post-conflict behavior," weirdest is "vocalized panting"—scrubbed of anything that might actually remind us of laughter. De Waal calls this nonhuman terminology "linguistic castration."[4]

I remain unsure how one is supposed to talk about the wild, the free, or even the captive and domesticated. I don't know what I am reasonably allowed to suppose or imagine. But that night, crouching on the carpet, looking at Coco through the dim, orange glow of the bedroom light, I could see that she was scared.

It was midnight. The next hour moved quickly. I woke up MC and called the vet's emergency number. Fortunately, there was always someone to pick up the phone, and the vet who answered told me he would meet us at the clinic. Allegra helped me put Coco, panting loudly, her svelte stomach visibly contracting and releasing, into a laundry basket. We drove to the clinic, and again, because of Covid protocols, I was not allowed inside. The young vet who had told me we were expecting two puppies took Coco's basket from me and told us to wait in the car.

The labor was proving complicated, the vet said when he reappeared half an hour later. Coco was a first-time mother and nervous. Initially, he suggested keeping her at the clinic so he could observe her. Then, a half hour later, he said she might be delaying labor out of anxiety and that we should take her home and come back if there was no delivery by 4:00 a.m. It was close to 2:00 a.m. by the time we were driving back to MC's cottage and, just as we pulled into the driveway, the birth began. Coco started to pace back and forth within the cramped laundry basket, biting the edges in pain, pushing with her whole body. I could see that the pup was in breech, coming out legs first. I had read several books on whelping and knew that though it wasn't ideal, a breech birth wasn't as problematic for dogs as for people and required only some gentle assistance to help the puppy be born safely. But still, I was nervous. The iron scent of blood filled the air.

For all Coco's straining, the puppy wasn't being pushed out. "Take her basket into the house," the vet advised on the phone, "you'll have to deliver the puppies. Slowly ease them out in tandem with her breathing, gently, as she exhales." Upstairs, in my better lit bedroom, I crouched on the floor close to Coco and whispered to her as I brought my hand toward her, but when my gloved fingers touched the unborn pup's wet, curled body, I felt bone but no flesh.

We got back in the car and drove through the dark, sleepy village to the clinic once more. Spiriting Coco away again, the vet reported to us there were not, as it turned out, two pups but one, and it was malformed. It was just skeleton and an oversize skull, and it was already dead. Because of her puppy's enlarged head, Coco would need to have a cesarean. In the parking lot, I was given a form to sign acknowledging that my dog might not survive the procedure and any liability and loss would be my own.

But by the time we had driven away and pulled up to the cottage once more, I got another call from the young vet. There had been no need for the cesarean. "Come back," the vet said on the phone, "you can collect her now." Coco had delivered her lifeless puppy naturally, and the vet, shaken by the experience, finally let me inside the clinic. Coco scrambled to get outside, away from him, from there, from everything. And for a moment, I thought she seemed fine, normal. "She won't remember this," MC and Allegra reassured me. "They don't feel the way we do. They're different." But that night, Coco slept in my bed and trembled nonstop, whimpering and moaning.

When a dog gives birth to a litter of puppies, she presides over them fully. Her stomach sheds hair so that they can suckle more easily, as she is their only source of food and nourishment for a month or more. She warms her young with her body and licks them in order to stimulate urination and defecation. If a mother rejects her pups, this stimulation has to be done by a human, with cotton wool and warm water; otherwise the newborn puppies can't expel waste. For the week after her stillbirth, Coco refused to leave my bed, clinging to me, shivering constantly. She growled and barked hysterically if anyone, even Allegra, whom she had loved since her own puppyhood, came into the room or approached us when we were together. Her appetite vanished; she could not be enticed to food, eating only what I ate if anything at all, lifting her head from my lap only long enough to take the food from my fingers before settling her head back down to chew.

When she started to lick my hand, I assumed it was for comfort. But then she started sleeping on it, holding it, caressing it, jumping to cover it whenever anyone opened the door or she heard voices approaching us. It was instinctual; she was a grieving mother.

I submitted my hand to Coco day after day and let her lick it until my skin was pink and raw. The vet was still unable to explain to me how he had failed to see that something was wrong—when Coco had had no enlarged stomach, pregnancy weight gain, prenatal kicking or squirming—or even how he had seen two heads and two hearts instead of one, or none. What he did tell me was that Coco wouldn't heal for as long as she thought my hand was a puppy, and that her body would keep producing milk, her hormones would be firing away, reacting to all her postnatal needs.

You have to take your hand away from her, the vet cautioned. I tried, but failed many times.

Chapter 4

If the covenant between humans and dogs is forty thousand years old, why does it feel trivial to me to speak of those bonds? Their beginnings are tied with wolves, with whom they share their social drive, animal instincts, physiognomy, anatomy, and 99.96 percent of their DNA.[5] As human beings we had contact with wolves long before we did much else. We interacted with them before we farmed, before we tilled land, before we became the industrious and organized creatures that we now are. It's suspected that wolves began to circle us as we produced food waste—they not only hunt but also scavenge, and all that delicious food would have eased their fear of us enough for them to come and pick through our garbage. And it was like this that an "accidental natural selection of wolves who are less fearful of humans would have begun."[6] The theory is that these more friendly, less skittish wolves were more scavengers than hunters and were the smaller and less alpha of their packs.

Using DNA analysis, scientists now know that dogs descended "almost entirely" from the Eurasian gray wolf, or *Canis lupus*.[7] Where they were domesticated is open to debate, as it happened so early in human history—before we domesticated any other animal, before cattle or sheep or pigs—that there is little available evidence. It was, experts wager, likely across Asia, perhaps the Middle East, and possibly in Europe. Why we domesticated gray wolves over foxes or jackals or other canids is probably down to luck: they just happened to be at the right place at the right time.

Over the years, humans began to adopt those smaller, doglike wolves and live with them as pets. Maybe they took them in as pups, and before they knew it, they were breeding these wolves, and so began the first part of domestication. It's said that the next part of this process would have been more deliberate: our ancestors got rid of or abandoned or destroyed the animals they didn't want living among them. The animals they kept, however, lost their more feral qualities, their more wolfish characteristics, and gave up hunting, pack living, and a strict observance of hierarchy.

While dogs and wolves are genetically almost indistinguishable, the biologist John Bradshaw has studied how vastly different their behavior is. Dogs are not pack animals in the way wolves are. When they do form packs, they are messy and less coherent than wolf packs, and they tend to prefer forming relationships with us over other dogs, although still friendly to them. Wolf packs go out of their way to avoid meeting not only people but wolves from other packs, too. When they happen to encounter each other, they "almost always fight, sometimes to the death."[8] Additionally, puppies are able to form dual identities at the very start of their lives—part human, part dog—in a way that wolf cubs are simply incapable of doing.[9]

Dogs kept some of their hierarchical instincts, replacing alpha wolves with their human masters. It was their ability to move between packs—leaving the pack they were born into to create their own pack once they had matured and found mates—that made them so perceptive and attentive to us. "The openness of these early wolf dogs," Alexandra Horowitz, a student of dogs, writes, "allowed them to adjust to a new pack, one that would include animals of an entirely different species."[10] She notes that dogs that are exposed to other animals—whether cats or wolves or horses or us— in their first few months of life form not just attachments but strong preferences for those species over any other. That bond is powerful enough to override their predatory or fear drives.

And they loved us as much as we loved them, pretty much from the start. And boy did we love them. There's evidence of puppies being nursed alongside human babies in Polynesia, Melanesia, and the Americas.[11] Aboriginals in Australia have a long history of taking dingo puppies from the wild to keep as companions purely based on their cuteness—we know this because the dingoes didn't help their masters in any particular way. On the contrary, they were kind of a nuisance—they stole food, made loads of noise, mated with other dingoes all the time, and besides, Aboriginal hunters found that they brought back more meat when they left their dingo pets at home than when they brought them along.[12] Archaeological evidence of dog skeletons curled up next to human remains in ancient grave sites stands as further proof that we domesticated dogs before any other animals—even cats. The first known dog burial dates back fourteen thousand years—the partial skeleton of a dog was found interred alongside two humans in Bonn-Oberkassel, Germany.[13] After which, dogs and humans being buried together became commonplace. Some other animals were laid to rest beside their humans along the way, but nothing close to how frequently we entombed our dogs with us.

We passed on so much of what is considered uniquely human to them too. Unlike wolves, who are exceedingly capable of independent problem solving, a dog will try to get its ball from under the couch for about a minute before it surrenders and comes to us for help. We gave them our desire for eye contact with intimates. Wolves take eye contact as threatening and avoid it because it signals a battle for authority. But dogs have evolved to look into our eyes for all sorts of cues: how we are feeling, what's going on, where the food is. Horowitz says this might even be "one of the first steps in the domestication of dogs: we chose those that looked at us."[14] In 2022, Japanese researchers found that dogs produced tears when reuniting with their humans.[15] It was eye contact that made us want to care for dogs, for when they looked at us and we looked back into their eyes, we released oxytocin, also known as the "bonding" or "love" hormone.

Language acquisition was long considered to be the exclusive domain of humans, but recent studies have shown that dogs can remember the names of their old toys even if they haven't seen them for years.[16] We know dogs know what words mean—how else would they sit and fetch and wag their tails when we tell them we're going to the park?—but a recent study found that dogs not only know the meanings of nouns, they know we are mistaken if we hold up a ball and call it a Frisbee.[17] There is so much we share between us that scientists note dogs are attuned to human gestures so intimately, they catch cues from us that even chimpanzees, our closest living relatives, miss.[18]

In a world of excess and power and all their rot, what besides love forces us to be pure? I feel numb for the first few weeks of lockdown, as though a formless nothingness has stretched over all my hours and days, but some things bring me immediately to tears. Shaheed Aitzaz Hassan Bangash, a fifteen-year-old Pakistani schoolboy, stopped a suicide bomber from entering his school, where the bomber would have killed two thousand students. When he saw the bomber, Aitzaz ran to him and embraced him, pushing him away from the school. Aitzaz was in the ninth grade when he gave his life to save others. I call this young man Shaheed, which means "martyr." I call him a martyr because he gave his life so others could live. I recite the names of our brave and defiant every day, like a rosary.

Another young man, Mashal Khan, a university student and poet, was lynched by a mob of fellow students who accused him of blasphemy. In Pakistan, there is no death sentence more inescapable—to describe an alleged act of blasphemy is to blaspheme, so accusers need not furnish their assertions with detail or proof. Just the accusation is enough. Mashal was tall and stocky, with a gentle, pensive face. In the photos that newspapers printed after his murder, he is often hunched over, a long shawl draped across his broad shoulders, looking far into the distance. Days after his son was buried, his father spoke to the Pakistani press. Mashal was beaten by his peers from ten in the morning till three in the afternoon. He called his son a humanist.

I carry these boys' names with me, keeping them close. On the anniversaries of their deaths, when I see their pictures, I mourn.

I check my Twitter routinely in the middle of the night and look at Instagram until I know an embarrassing amount about utter strangers. I start to post about animal cruelty, about what seem like daily failures of compassion. I follow a few shelters in Pakistan and am deluged with heart-stopping videos and pictures of the dark things people do to animals. Torture, abuse, abandonment; too many pictures, too much pain.

Glory to the hands that labor, the Puerto Rican poet and anti-imperialist activist Juan Antonio Corretjer wrote in his famous poem "Oubao Moin." I am haunted by the thought of Indian migrant workers on death marches from cities to rural homes, where they will go into lockdown and their families will starve; the Pakistani farmers who are forced to throw entire harvests away because of government price gouging; and American prison populations laid waste to by the virus. Though I know it's not the case, it feels like every day of this interminable year comes with a portent of horror. In January, in the new year that still feels very much like the old, gunmen enter a coal mine near the town of Mach, Balochistan, and identify ten ethnic Hazaras. Hazaras originally hail from central Afghanistan, though over time they have migrated from the mountains down into Pakistan and Iran. Besides being ethnically and linguistically unique, Hazaras are Shias and so have been marginalized and perse-cuted by Sunni-led groups like the Taliban in Afghanistan and right-wing fundamentalists in Pakistan. They are very distinct looking, beautiful, with Asiatic features and light eyes. You can spot them in a crowd, just like the gunmen did. They marched the men out of the mine, took them to a mountaintop, and killed them. After their murders, their families sat in the bitter cold and grieved, waiting for the prime minister, Imran Khan, to come and mourn with them. But the prime minister was too busy meeting YouTubers and Turkish television producers. He wouldn't come.

The mourners defied Islamic convention and, in protest, refused to bury their dead, holding fast to the bodies of their loved ones, waiting. Still, the prime minister refused. He stated that he would not be "blackmailed."[19]

"What kind of times are these," Brecht asked in a poem written just before the start of World War II, "when to talk about trees is almost a crime because it implies silence about so many horrors?"[20] The voices reprimand me. Why are you sitting in the middle of nowhere—in gardens and forests with dogs—and writing about animals and a gaslighter only a fool would have believed? Explain yourself. Be true.

Did I tell you all the above so you will think I'm serious too?

When my brother Zulfikar was young, we had a deer, a fawn, that through a series of events had come to live in our garden. We called her Bambi. She ate leaves from the palms of our hands. When Zulfikar walked in the garden, talking to the champa trees and flowers, the fawn shadowed him. She loved him the way that a boy needs to be loved: softly. Never imposing or intruding, but always near him. One day Zulfikar's mother, my stepmother, tired of the damage done to her plants, and sent the deer away, donating Bambi to the Karachi Zoo. I don't remember why we didn't know and why we couldn't stop her. I suppose because we were children. I remember only how upset my brother was, how painfully hurt. Zulfikar had a special love for all animals. He would rescue bats that had flown into the bright reflective glass of our dining room window; he treated birds with injured wings and cried, sobbed, whenever animals in films were hurt. The zoo called us soon after, the deer—perfectly healthy—had died. Just like that, one day, out of nowhere. Of a broken heart, they said.

My parents divorced when I was three. I didn't have any relationship with my mother; my father was my sole parent, guardian, and caretaker. When I was seven years old, he remarried, and though for a while my stepmother and I were close, no one came near the universe my father and I inhabited. My stepmother was also someone who could be complicated and calculating. Because I had been grief-struck as a young girl, my attachment to her—which was connected to so many of my fears and traumas over the violence that had demarcated my young life—was completely blind to many of her faults. Even though I was savvy and alert on other fronts, hypervigilant to signs of danger or violence, observant of the minutiae around me, and never trustful of anyone, when it came to the fragility of my own life, my guard was so far down, I let a lot of manipulations pass me by. I was so worried people I loved would be hurt and so protective of others, that I left myself completely exposed.

Suffice it to say, I was well schooled by a narcissist long before I met the man. Though I have a strong character myself, I had also been trained in appeasement, ready to surrender any battle if my loved ones are remotely threatened. The man and my stepmother were similar in more ways than one, and both used this fear I had of harm coming to people I loved, my deepest fear, to make sure I never questioned either of them too much. Losing my father had made me terrified of abandonment. Without him, I felt forsaken. It was my duty to make sure no one else left, to make sure everyone else was safe, if only to stave off total desolation for myself. My stepmother often reminded me that she was in danger thanks to her association with our family; in her mind, she was as valuable a target as my father had been. More, even. The man had a similar carte blanche: he knew he could do anything he liked; I would accept any behavior rather than risk his leaving.

My father never thought he would live long, and though he promised me he would do everything in his power to accompany me through life, he never lied to me. If I asked him not to go somewhere or do something or not to pick some political fight, he gently but firmly reminded me that he had a duty to others that superseded his duty to me. I knew from a young age that Papa did not exaggerate, and so I understood even as a child how vulnerable both he and I were: one day he wouldn't be there anymore. I only prayed that day would come late. But when it came, much sooner than I could have prepared for, I lost my sole anchor in the world. Without my father, who would protect me? I saw it as my mission then to protect my brother Zulfikar, but in my mind, I was all but alone in the world. My stepmother and, later, the man were there, but neither unconditionally. Their presence in my life was dependent on how I behaved with them, more precisely on how much I was willing to give, and they reminded me of this with surprising regularity. "One day, I won't be here anymore," the man sighed if I disagreed with him or we argued, "and you'll see how much I was trying to protect/help/guide you."

"Fuck you!" my stepmother screamed at me at the lunch table when I asked her a question about money, specifically why I couldn't handle my own finances and actually see the accounts that had come in that day. "I saved your life after your father was killed and this is the thanks I get?" She threatened to leave the house and stormed out of the room, slamming the door shut until I relented and said, Okay, okay, I didn't need to see the accounts.

Let sleeping dogs lie, that's what I learned from my step-mother. Sometimes it was better, easier, not to know. I had been left enough times to surrender quickly when faced with the possibility of another person vanishing.

I am not a confessional writer, and I have had my privacy violated enough for one lifetime, had enough intrusion, speculation, and endless interventions from strangers because of the unusual circumstances of my life. It burns to think of myself as weak. I spent so long, it feels like all my life, fighting forces so much larger than myself. I have only ever wanted to be fearless, no matter the tremors of my many, many fears.

Deep down I know that I am writing this book because for periods, long periods, I was isolated in controlling relationships. I was not able to tell anyone about either my stepmother or the man for a very long time, because I wanted to protect them but also largely because I never thought someone like me, strong-willed and independent, could be in danger of entrapment. I wanted to be strong so much I convinced myself that those relationships were normal, acceptable. What I deserved. And I willfully ignored the fact that I should have been concerned with protecting myself rather than them. I felt so insecure in the world after my father was killed that, without realizing it, I clung to anyone who appeared strong. I didn't know how I could survive life alone and sought reassurance, desperately, hopefully, from those I thought I could trust.

Vivian Gornick's *Fierce Attachments* gave me the first insight I had that you can love a mother who is poisonous. If I had read something about coercive relationships during the years that I was with the man, I might have been knocked out of my fantasy for long enough to ask myself some distressing questions. But even though I read voraciously and had done so since I was a child, I missed a glimmer of light into what kinds of relationships need darkness in order to bloom.

I wish someone had told me that when a man asks you to keep a secret, you should change your phone number and move towns to avoid having anything to do with him ever again. Rather, I understood secrets as being necessary to survival. You didn't tell people your movements, you kept your schedule to yourself, you changed it every day, and when others knew too much about you, you were required to recalibrate and reorder things to maintain a certain physical safety for yourself. So when this pattern emerged in my relationship, I consented. Tragicomically, in trying to escape my controlling, suffocating stepmother, I launched myself headfirst into another coercive relationship. I was an adult, and there's plenty I should have known about love—how it works and how it betrays us—but did not. I had plenty of failures of my own.

At that time, I had a dog, Lama, a long-haired dachshund, who loved me more than I was able to love back. I hid from her sometimes because it overwhelmed me how much she needed me. First, I was close to her and she would sleep every night in my bed, and then I was not, traveling for work and life and making my distance from home greater and greater in pursuit of freedom but also of the man whom I believed loved me even though he was often harsh with me. To ease the heartsickness of that necessary distance, I retreated from my Karachi friends and my old life. When I came home from my trips, I wouldn't call anyone for weeks, sitting alone in my room and working. When I traveled, I didn't keep in touch. I was preparing to leave my family home, but I didn't realize how, at times, I was unkind. One night, I arrived from the airport late and went straight to the annex where I lived. In the dark cold of my bedroom, the air conditioner on full blast, I was unpacking when I heard Lama scratching at the door. She had heard the car and felt me return. I listened, even as she whined for me, but I didn't let her in that night. I was trying to sever my ties to home; I wanted so much to leave I didn't know how else to do it but to vanish without notice or apology. I just closed my eyes and put on a podcast so I wouldn't hear Lama whimpering at the door. Eventually she left and I went to sleep.

She died three months later, when I was away again. I don't forgive myself for my coldness to her. When she died, I was inconsolable, though I had been so unfeeling to Lama when I was trying to carve myself away. I knew I had not been good to her, not been just, and now I would have no way to redeem myself. I cried for her, for what that rejection must do to an animal whose heart is so large, and for me, ashamed that I was capable of such pettiness. "Lama hasn't gone," the man told me. I thought of him as my best friend then, thought of him as wise and insightful. "You have a bond together"—he didn't know what I had done—"and that bond means she will return to you in some form or another. Watch for it. Wait for her."

I didn't believe him. But nine months later I got Coco. Do I feel something returned in her? I do. It is a full, large-hearted, forgiving love. I don't want to let it down this time. Not this time, not ever again. What, I ask myself over and over, do we owe the wild? Everything. At least, much more than we are willing to give.

Chapter 5

When I was little, my father and I had a nighttime routine: in the dark quiet of our Damascus flat, after reading me a bedtime storybook or inventing a tale of his own, he would sit beside my bed, pulling his chair close, and smoke his Rothmans cigarettes quietly until I fell asleep. He would kiss my forehead and whisper to me: "If anything ever happened to you, I would die." I remember so many of those nights, my eyes closing with sleep and dreams, listening to my father's warm voice. "Me too, Papa," I would faithfully reply. "I would die without you too." We spoke that oath to each other as easily as other people say "Sweet dreams."

By the time I was old enough to read along with my father, he had lost his own father and his younger brother to violent deaths. His father had been overthrown and assassinated by a military dictator, while his brother was only twenty-seven years old when he was poisoned. His mother and older sister remained in Pakistan and were both carted between jail and long periods of house arrest ordered by the junta. What remained of my father's family was scattered in exile, us in Syria and his younger sister in London. But Papa's bedtime oath to me was not born of those tragedies; he was not a maudlin man. He told me he would die without me not because his life had been struck by devastation or because he was sorrowful, but because it was true. Because my father was devoted to me and I to him. My world in its totality was reflected in him, nothing outside his orbit existed to me. Even in my young years, I never found his nighttime promise sad or heavy, because I loved my father more than anything, more than everything, on God's earth.

Papa loved life. He lived every moment to the absolute fullest. He played Motown music at full volume in the car, he sang and danced to Harry Belafonte, he drove too fast when it was late at night and the roads were clear, he went swimming every day that the sun was out, and he had an infectious laugh. He was fearless, just like I wanted to be. When I was thirteen and a dentist put hideous braces on my lower teeth, Papa told me I looked like Jaws, the James Bond villain. And when I cried, he got up from what he was doing and went to the car so we could go back to the dentist to have them taken off. I had to be the responsible one and sniffle, between tears, that I would keep them on, that the braces were for my own good.

*   *   *

In a life of violence and exile and danger, it was my father's love that sustained me. Whatever happened to us, we were *lucky*, my father told me again and again, so very lucky. That was his abiding sentiment: gratitude. We had each other and that was enough to survive anything life could throw at us.

The night he was killed, I came home alone from the clinic where his body lay, and I wrote down everything that had happened so I would never forget it, so in the pain and grief that followed I would never lose even the tiniest detail of my father's last hours on earth. I wrote it all down and I said goodbye. Goodbye not to my father but to my life, to who I was and to everything around me. For a while, I let myself be carried by the pain. It swept over the shards of what remained and would carry me toward my father eventually. But when it didn't, and I grew exhausted from acting and pretending that I was strong and fine and could survive what had happened, I fell into a long depression. The injustice of my father's murder debilitated me. I walked through every day in a trance somewhere between fury and grief. As I grew older, I was accompanied not by sadness but by anxiety, a shuddering, constant wave of panic and distress, but by then I was a good actress, and for the most part, I made it through without too many people noticing. And then, fourteen years after my father's death, on a book tour devoted to him, the story of his life and assassination, I lost my voice.

I woke up one morning, in London, where I was due to have several events, and couldn't speak. I wasn't in pain, but I couldn't get much out beyond a whisper. And when I tried, my throat felt coated in fire. Doctors couldn't find anything wrong with me, I had no infection, no vocal tearing. Friends gave me lozenges and teas and silver colloidal spray, but for as long as I was touring with *Songs of Blood and Sword*, my voice wouldn't stay. I would get through my talks and events and return to whatever hotel I was in and crumple. I calmly relived the worst moment of my life on a stage day after day but would sob if I couldn't find a charger for my phone or if a café was out of soy milk. I spent days alone in unlit rooms, unable to speak to anyone or get dressed or eat, hiding from a pain that followed me everywhere, every waking hour of the day. My voice faltered and vanished, it would come and go over the next year until, one day, traveling once again to speak about the book, I met the man.

Chapter 6

There is no brighter star in the night sky than the Dog Star, or Sirius. Its name comes from the old Greek word for "glowing," and it sits in the Canis Major or Greater Dog constellation. Sirius and Sirius B, its white dwarf companion star, also known as the pup, orbit each other in constant motion. Sirius is more luminous than the sun; sometimes, it is the brightest object of all, depending on if the moon and planets like Venus and Jupiter are below the horizon. Canis Major was known to the Ancient Greeks as Orion the Hunter's Dog. But according to the myth, Zeus gave Laelaps, the fastest dog in the universe, to Europa as a gift. Laelaps's destiny was not only to be the fastest but also to catch anything he chased or hunted. After Europa's husband, Cephalus, accidentally killed her with her javelin, Laelaps went to live with him. Cephalus took Laelaps to Thebes to catch a pesky fox that had been bothering the locals, but there was one problem: the fox's destiny was never to be caught. As the dog whose destiny was to catch anything it desired and the fox whose fate was forever to be free ran around in mad circles, Zeus grew irritated and cast them both into stone and into the night sky to live forever in the lights of Canis Major.

Canis Major is one of three dog constellations, informally known as Canis Major, the big dog; Canis Minor, the little dog; and Canes Venatici, the hunting dogs. But Sirius is the star of all the astral bodies. Sailors charting the Pacific Ocean used its light to find their way through the vast, fathomless waters. Ancient Egyptians predicted when their mighty river would flood its banks by watching for the reappearance of Sirius, and long ago, the Greeks knew summer had arrived when they sighted it. The Greeks also believed Sirius's arrival created a certain madness that caused dogs to become ill and even die. This dramatic phenomenon had a physiological rather than mystical explanation: the dogs *were* crazed, but by dehydration; they were heatstruck. The first heliacal rising of the Dog Star, with which both the ancient Greeks and Romans marked the blazing summer months, tended to occur at the start of July—the following forty days, what came to be known as the dog days, were the hottest period of the year.

The Sirius set of stars is the fifth closest stellar system to us on earth. When I was still a teenager, I used to look for it and claimed its presence as proof that my father was nearby. Wherever I was, it reassured me that I was not as alone as I felt. The Alaskan Inuit indigenous to the Bering Strait call Sirius the "moon dog." The Native Americans, notably the tribes of the Southwest like the Seri, and the Tohono O'odham, as well as the Cherokee Nation, know it by dog names, though the Skidi tribe of Nebraska call it the "wolf star." In Chinese astrology, it is the "celestial wolf." You can find reference to Sirius in the Koran in a sura named An-Najm, a collection of verses that calls on Muslims to fall to the earth, to bend in submission before God. In Sanskrit, the Dog Star is known as the deer hunter. These talismans—the deer, the dogs, wolves, the stars— followed me. They were everywhere.

When we met, the man didn't want anything from me. He wasn't intimidated by me; in contrast to almost everyone I encountered, he was preternaturally cool, unruffled, unfazed. He was curious about me, he told me, because he saw I was suffering and he knew he could fix it. He could see it from miles away, etched all over my face, telegraphed through everything I said and did. It was so simple to fix, he declared, it was a mystery that I hadn't seen how. "Take the pain away forever?" I had asked him, incredulous. "You won't even remember this sadness," he swore. "I can make it so you'll smile when you think of the worst moments of your life; they'll be gone, erased."

The man spoke to me gently about my pain, taught me to think of it in new terms, to see it in a different light, one that made it possible for me to forgive those who had caused me so much damage. Forgive them for yourself, he told me, not for them. Perhaps it is ironic that he taught me how to forgive, but he showed me it was possible, more than possible; it was easy, and it was necessary. Without me saying a word, he knew the worst things I had ever thought and felt. He knew them because he had, in his own life, felt them too. But he was free of them now, and it would be possible, he promised, for me to be liberated too. All I had to do was believe him. And I did. And it worked.

My sore throat vanished and my voice came back; I had fewer of those dark days that forced me to retreat into my room, and my panic attacks all but stopped. The man had a wild confidence, a surety about everything he said that made you believe him too, as outlandish as some of his claims were—that he could take away pain, remove suffering, proffer insight into any problem, no matter how large or how small. During our time together, I relied on him the way a student does a teacher or a patient their doctor. Any problem or worry I had, he would know how to fix. I ran to him for help all the time—and he did help me. He made my troubles go away. "Let me think about it," he'd say if he didn't have a solution immediately, and whatever ailed me would churn over in his mind until he returned with an answer, which he always did.

He taught me to walk in the dark on a moonless night by showing me how my eyes would eventually adjust to the black that surrounded me. When they did, he made me close my eyes so I couldn't rely on the glow from the stars above. "Use your feet," he said, "feel the earth." He walked me down the countryside hill we were on and up again with my eyes shut and feet bare. I sometimes felt he was teaching me how to survive without him, an act of kindness on his part. When we heard a rustling, a family of foxes or perhaps wild boars lurking in the night, he kept me walking. "Don't be afraid. They can tell if you're afraid."

He considered himself an outspoken feminist, though of course he would never use the term to describe himself, even as he often held forth on the rights of women. He didn't believe in equality per se; it was a construct, an imaginary concept that people didn't fully understand. But the man understood it instinctively; as someone drawn to Buddhist thought he was intimately familiar with all the fractures and failings of the self. Women had so many strengths, so many ways in which they contributed to politics and society, he often expounded, and they were so vital to the health of any community, family, or collective. He had many stories in his personal archive of all the women he had helped stand up for themselves, empowering them by engaging and guiding them. He helped me to stand up for myself with other people, insisting I confront them and have uncomfortable conversations in order not to be pushed around. He delighted in his ability to deliver powerful insights to strangers just as he had helped me with my grief.

The most significant events in our private, intimate lives can never be spoken about with strangers, except in books, the writer and memoirist Edmund White once wrote.

My life had been broken by grief, and then, for a period, it was redeemed by love. But people do not love each other in the same way, and sometimes there is terror in love. I wanted a family more than anything in the world. The man didn't. But instead of acknowledging that we wanted different things and that we might be better off in pursuit of such separate lives, we stayed together. It is difficult to look back now and see that I tolerated this for as long as I did. Some men take strong women as a challenge and derive a pleasure in breaking them—or trying to. And when you are a strong woman, you also might not think this can happen to you—that you might be in trouble, that someone you care for might be dangerous to you.

Even before meeting the man, I had built up a toxic self-esteem and sense of self-worth from proving to myself that I could survive anything, withstand any pain, any trauma, endure it, and keep going. I had dealt with manipulative and cruel people before, and when I saw the first glimmer of those qualities in him, very early in our being together, I thought I could survive him too.

Once, on our way to dinner, he decided he wanted to pop into a speaker store to fiddle with the electronics. This was one of the man's favorite pastimes, whiling away hours in shops he had no actual interest in. I had learned that if I resisted these diversions, they lasted twice as long. I was hungry but paced quietly behind him as he asked the salesman technical questions about sound or wattage or whatever it is that makes speakers loud. "Where are you from, my brother?" the man asked the salesman. "Egypt," he replied. He must have been in his thirties, a youngish guy who took pride in his uniform. His trousers were ironed perfectly, his shoes shined, and his manner courteous.

"Egypt, nice. She speaks Arabic." The man pointed at me as he walked past another device. The salesman said something to me, and I replied that I understood it better than I spoke. It had been a long time since I had lived in the Middle East.

The man continued his browsing and asking questions that only the person who invented speakers could have reasonably answered. At one point, the salesman was about to offer some advice—"If you and your wife—" but the man interrupted him. "Her?" His face curled into a grimace. "She's not my wife." He said it as though he had taken offense. I braced myself, waiting for the joke that was sure to follow. "Oh sorry, if you and your girlfriend—" the salesman started again. But again, the man interrupted him.

"Oh no no *no*, she's not my girlfriend," he corrected the salesman. "Please. We're not together. You like her? Ask her out." And with that, the man sauntered off to look at another speaker.

The polite salesman didn't know what to say. He looked back and forth between us. "Is he serious?" he asked me in Arabic.

My face burnt with shame. At that moment, looking at the man, his hands clasped comfortably behind his back, shoulders slightly hunched as he stared at one nearly identical speaker after another, I couldn't stand the sight of him. "No," I replied. "He's not being serious. He's being awful."

"Why would he say that?" the salesman asked me softly, still in Arabic, his face puzzled. I shrugged. I was so embarrassed. I just wanted to leave the shop, the man, this ugly moment, and disappear. "If I had a girlfriend like you," the saleman continued, "I would never talk like that." I smiled at him. I didn't know what else to do, how else to thank a stranger for being kind. "Never," he repeated before he walked away from me, shaking his head.

This happened other times, cabbies said similar things to me—"he doesn't treat you right, love"—and I saw the faces of many bystanders as the man threw scenes and tantrums in countless public places. More important, *I* knew. I didn't need anyone to tell me how miserable he often made me feel. But in response, I simply ignored everything and pushed down every painful memory; I could survive it. It was just words. I had been through worse. I generously allowed myself an almost complete amnesia about the man. He was special, I told myself. This was special.

On one of our first trips together, we spent a few days in Paris. At night, after dinner, we walked around the city and he taught me ridiculous but effective methods of self-defense, such as if a man attacks you, pretend you're into it and lean in to kiss him but gouge his eyes out with your thumbs and bite his face instead. He held forth on Buddhism, industrial history, World War II, the Mongols, and counterespionage tactics.

He taught me how to walk against the howling wind and protect myself against the cold, how to catch and free fireflies, and—with great resistance on my part—how to ride a motorcycle. He seemed to have an almost adolescent obsession with disaster-laden scenarios and experienced the world as a set of permanent crises, extreme dramas, and threats to evade. But at the time, I didn't notice that. Instead, captivated, I listened.

One afternoon, lying across the bed on his back, he posed what I misunderstood to be a simple question: "Do you want to have a normal or a special relationship?" he asked me in a soft voice. Paris was growing dark and quiet outside, as though the trains at nearby Gare du Nord had stopped in their tracks and the noise of honking Vespas was suddenly turned off; there was only the vague static of silence and the hum of the hotel's central cooling system. "What's the difference?" I asked.

"A normal relationship is like all the others; it'll be nice and you'll be happy but it won't be extraordinary."

"And the special kind?"

"It'll be the greatest love you've ever known," he said sadly, "but also the greatest pain." One hand was folded across his chest as he spoke, and I lay my head against his other arm. The special kind, I answered.

"Are you sure?" he asked me. He was calm but spoke in a deliberate and considered tone. I was.

I wanted him more than anything else at the time and thought the answer was easy. But looking back, I ask myself, Why did I just accept the promise of pain without any resistance? I had been so lucky in life, so lucky that I understood pain, tragedy, and even violence, to some degree, to be my comeuppance.

I thought it was my karma, a curse of sorts: I had never felt true, gnawing hunger, always had a roof over my head, and until my father was taken from me, I had been deeply loved. For these privileges, why shouldn't God or the universe, or whatever divine force there was, exact a price? When I was younger, I often tried to find a sequence to suffering, counting the years between violent deaths to see if there was a pattern. But as far as I could calculate, it was too random to determine, and I didn't know enough math to arrive at a reliable average of when exactly those you loved would be ripped away from you. Maybe these were the costs to a lucky life, I often thought, when the man fulfilled his warning to me about the greatest pain he would deliver. I was grateful for everything I had been given, but why shouldn't things be taken from me too?

Many years later, a friend trying to help me make sense of my catastrophic lapses of judgment quoted Proust: when we are in love, we love nothing else. But Proust didn't quite say that. What he said was something altogether more tragic: "When we are in love, our love is too big a thing for us to be able altogether to contain it within ourselves. It radiates towards the loved one, finds there a surface which arrests it, forcing it to return to its starting-point, and it is this repercussion of our own feeling which we call the other's feelings and which charms us more then than on its outward journey because we do not recognise it as having originated in ourselves."[21] Proust also noted that love is a great sign of how little reality actually matters to us.

In the calculus of my lost decade, I am shocked by how little reality mattered to me. When the man told me to stop wearing jewelry—even small earrings or sentimental objects, nothing of any actual value—I believed that this was the practice of someone fascinated with Buddhism and antimaterial thought. Similarly, when he told me not to buy so many books, to give all mine away and empty my bookshelves, and that I mustn't wear makeup because it made me look like a mouse with eyeliner on, my alarm bells weren't activated and I didn't question why he was trying to control me. Anytime I mentioned that I had a dinner or event to attend, he would ignore my calls and messages before said event, calling me exactly at the time he knew I'd be out. If I answered, he would be sweet and chatty, acting as though I wasn't surrounded by people. "Please talk to me," he'd cajole, "I was missing you." If I didn't answer his call, he'd text me with rising ire. "Are you too busy for me? Got something more important to do?"

When he suggested that certain friends of mine might not wish me well or that I may want to cleave some new distance between me and my group of girlfriends, I didn't like it and tried to ignore it, but his insistent advice got under my skin. He had been right about other things, after all. He had been right when he swore that there was a way to ease grief or when he insisted that meditation stills the terrifyingly constant anxieties of the mind. I brushed off his commentary on my writing and friends, not willing to sacrifice either, just like I tuned out of conversations with girlfriends who told me about emotionally abusive relationships, figuring they were talking about themselves. They didn't know about him anyway, so they couldn't have known about the many humiliations and degradations he put me through because I had not yet learned how to deal with his complex personality. Besides, those things just didn't happen to women like me.

I had never seen anything like his temper before, never encountered someone so volatile or unpredictable. Over time I became alert to the warning signs: he would fall ominously silent and physically withdraw, even if it was as slight a movement as sitting back in his chair or removing his elbows from the table to fold his arms across his chest. His eyes would narrow till his pupils were dark and heavy. If he was seriously about to explode, he sometimes repeated something you had said back to you—both confirming what you had said *and* giving you the chance to incriminate yourself further. "Oh, you think I have a hard time sharing my feelings with my parents?" Once he had expended his rage, he would go back to normal, as though nothing had happened. He very rarely apologized for his outbursts. Why should he? Should you have to go through life apologizing simply because people were sensitive and didn't know how the real world worked? Often, he excused himself by reminding me that shouting was the only way he could get through to me. It was my fault, I was stubborn, I didn't listen. When I fought back, the man's voice would chill and his eyes would go glassy. "You want to fight?" he would ask me slowly. "Are you trying to make me angry?"

He thought writing was a quaint profession. He admired that I took it seriously, but he also thought that he understood writing better than I—and most other writers—did because he had no ego, nothing to prove to anyone, no insecurities. When my first novel was longlisted for the Baileys Women's Prize for Fiction, my stepmother wondered how it would look in Pakistan to be nominated for a prize named after a liqueur. Perhaps I ought to remove myself from the running? And the man shrugged his shoulders and said, "Hmm, oh yeah?" before changing the topic to something more important. When I tried to explain that it was actually quite exciting for a debut novelist, he told me I had no right to tell him how to react to anything and didn't speak to me for the rest of the day. He refused to read my books on the grounds that if he did he would know too much about me and uncharacteristically professed that this was too much power for him to have.

But the world around him was just as mercurial as he was, and somehow, exactly at the moments when I found him oppressive or controlling, he would drop his guard ever so dramatically and I would witness him suffer personal defeats with a kind of grace he rarely displayed to me. It was magnetic. And when I made him laugh or smile, I felt I had lifted some burden from his shoulders, and I wanted to do it again and again. If I did, maybe he would be different, maybe he would be happy.

Because he was stingy with his praise or his compliments, I simply worked harder for them. Because it took so long for him to say "I love you," I wanted it more. "You always want me to tell you I love you," he said once, trimming his nails in a hotel room, "because you think it means I won't leave you." He stood by a windowsill, his eyes narrowing on his task. "But I won't ever leave you, it can't happen." He still wasn't looking at me. I was standing by the doorframe, watching him. "It's impossible."

It never occurred to me to interpret this as a threat.

What was I getting out of it?

I stayed much longer than I should have, in part because I wanted a child. It was my strongest desire, and without my wanting it to, it shaped everything I thought about the man and allowed me to idealize him while excusing his many flaws. The man knew this.

And because he told me it would happen, but only if I was patient, I made a terrible pact with him. I would wait for him to be ready, and if I did, he swore he would give me a child. "You can't force these things, you have to wait for the right time," he insisted. To me, it made no sense at our age to carry on a relationship with someone for years and years only not to settle down and start a family. But the man dismissed these concerns. Relax, he would drawl in a voice intended to convey that I was overreacting, what are you so worked up about? Didn't I believe in him? I did. Then? Then what? Then why are you worrying? Don't nag me. It'll happen when it happens. If it's meant to be, nothing in the world will be able to stop it. Can't you see what I'm going through? We are meant to be together. I'll never let you go. Have faith. This was a special relationship. What could go wrong?

Chapter 7

One day, my brother told me the story of Imam Reza, the eighth Shia Imam and descendant of the Prophet Mohammad (peace be upon him), who is known as Zamin-e-Ahu, or the guarantor of the deer. Islam has many of these stories of animals and humans. I remember being told that when man first walked the earth, all the birds flew high into the sky and the fish deep into the sea, terrified, because they knew the destroyer of the world had arrived. According to Islam, on Judgment Day, animals will be called upon to testify how you treated them. The Koran dedicates whole surahs or chapters to ants and bees, and mentions animals in two hundred verses, sometimes as warnings or admonishments. But still, it is hard to forget that it was a spider, a tiny insect, that saved the Prophet's life from his enemies, weaving its web over the entrance of a cave where he had sought refuge from attack.

Though I was mostly quiet about the longings that I carried as the man dragged our relationship on through my late thirties, somehow, my brother appeared with stories exactly at the time I needed them most. On his journey from Madina to Khurasan, Imam Reza was walking through a jungle when he saw a hunter poised to kill a deer. The deer had been on her way to feed her young when the hunter trapped her. Without their mother's milk, the fawns would die. Please, the deer begged Imam Reza, let me feed my children, and when I am done, I will come back to be taken by the hunter and killed. Imam Reza stood as guarantor for the deer's promise and told the hunter he would wait alongside him. Though no one thought she would return, the deer—honorable animals that deer are—came back with her fawns and duly presented herself for death. The hunter was so shocked, and so shamed, that he put down his weapon. The deer would live.

When my brother told me this story, I realized I had forgotten something fundamental. That cruelty can be interrupted, that men can be shamed, that decency and surrender can bring an end to suffering, rather than invite more of it. These parables and legends and stories were the only things—alongside the lessons taught to me by my small, hysterical dog—that broke through my isolation. I didn't always understand why these stories affected me so much, but they stayed with me, they lingered in my thoughts. Pay attention, I told myself. Something is trying to speak to you. How can we ever be forgiven the debt we owe the creatures of the wild?

When we had been together nearly five years, the man and I traveled to Sardinia for a weeklong summer vacation with his cousin and his partner. We stayed in a small cabin near the sea, in a block of resort-style cabins chosen by his relative. There was nothing to do but swim and play bocce on the beach. The cabin had no Wi-Fi or television. In the evenings and mornings, we would walk to the beach bar with our phones and iPads to check our mail and download movies to watch at night. The man and I didn't argue.

We passed our time at restaurants, eating fresh fish and pasta, and going to the supermarket to find things to grill on the rickety cabin barbecue. Once or twice a day, we would go swimming. I was happy in the water, wading and floating close to the shore while he rented paddleboards and Jet Skis to entertain himself. In the back of his cousin's car on the way to dinner, toward the end of the trip, he told me the way I applied concealer—patting it lightly under my eyes—looked stupid. I ignored the comment. He continued to inform me the shade wasn't right for me. I ignored that too, he was not a beauty consultant. But that night, he also told me he liked my dress. It was a rare compliment.

The restaurant was small, its walls painted lavender, with little vases of wildflowers on all the tables. The man and I sat side by side. We ate red prawn, only lightly seared. The man was in a good mood. He flicked food at me, rolling the soft flesh of bread into little balls and aiming them at my cheek. Turning in my seat to face him, I batted the projectile balls away, but he wouldn't stop. His phone was on the table, so I grabbed it, holding it in the air like a shield. I laughed and said, "If you don't stop, I'm taking your phone hostage."

In a split second, in an almost knee-jerk reaction, the man grabbed my left pinkie finger and bent it back. "Give me my phone."

"No," I replied, shocked that he was willing to hurt me just to get his phone back. But shock gave way to anger. *What was on the phone?*

My finger was bent so far back that my skin began to turn white. I couldn't move out of his grip.

I made a small noise not unlike laughter but also not unlike a cry. Still, I didn't lower his phone. His cousin stood up to go to the bathroom. His partner sat and watched us blankly. Neither of them tried to intervene.

"You're hurting me."

"Too bad," he replied, his face tight and expressionless.

I began to cry. I dropped his phone onto the table. "I guess you have a lot to hide," I said, through tears. His cousin suggested we go to a gelateria nearby for ice cream and asked for the check.

The man apologized, likely only because he was embarrassed that his cousin and partner had witnessed this even though they were reacting as if nothing out of the ordinary had happened.

"Don't cry," he said in a singsong voice I hadn't heard before, "you'll make me upset."

In the back of the car, the man tried to hug me. I didn't let him. I didn't want to be near him. At the gelateria, he bought me ice cream—a rare gesture of generosity—but I refused it. He stroked my hair. "I got carried away. I went too far."

My brother once wrote a poem about Joseph (of the dream coat, and son of Jacob). In it, Joseph dreams of eleven stars that bow to him and lead him out of loneliness and toward freedom.

Remembering the poem years later, I tried but failed to find the story of Joseph's stars and solitude in the Bible. I found stories of jealousy (his brothers resentfully assumed they were the stars whose submission had been foretold in Joseph's dream) and others of prophecy (the stars were symbols of divine love, a love that foretold the coming of Christ), but I found nothing on lighting a path out of solitude. I looked for signs and answers everywhere, hunting for some light that would ease the uncertainty that continued to haunt me. Maybe I wouldn't have the love story I had prayed for, maybe it wouldn't end well, maybe I wouldn't be a mother. Maybe there was something I was supposed to know about the world that I hadn't understood yet. Maybe life was a gift and I misunderstood it as sorrow.

In the end, I didn't have eleven stars that led me out of loneliness. But looking back, I see that I did have a few portents.

The first: I had a second novel to finish and I couldn't think anywhere, so I bought a ticket to Seville, and Coco and I arrived with a carry-on suitcase filled with notebooks and dog food. We were alone. In the mornings, we had our breakfast of *pan con tomate* and coffee on a café terrace and then returned to our small hotel to work. Before and after dinner, I walked Coco in the grand gardens of what was once the capital of Al-Andalus, Ishbiliya, as Seville is known in Arabic. Al-Andalus, a pinnacle of Muslim art, architecture, and culture, was the farthest west that Muslim warriors had traveled at the time, less than a hundred years after Islam was born in the deserts of Arabia. Tariq bin Ziyad, a freedman and a Berber, landed his forces in Spain and claimed the land in the name of Damascus's Umayyad rulers. The Arabs didn't settle Spain—most of Al-Andalus became Muslim by conversion. I knew little then about the Arab conquest of Spain. But there, in Seville, walking among the palm trees that reminded me of my childhood in Syria, I saw Damascus everywhere.

Seville is a city fragrant with the warm perfume of orange blossoms, the starbursts of wild jasmines growing in thickets, the earthy smell of horses clip-clopping on the cobble streets. We spent four days there. I delighted in the architecture of my childhood, the soft, bubbling fountains, the celebration of water, of all life's origins, the ornate courtyards swelling with flowers, the elegant lions whose visages are sculpted with thick manes and who are placed at vantage points around the gardens and castles as sentinels. For someone who has spent her life homesick, the discovery of Andalucia was a treasure. I looked up all the old Arab names of Spanish cities: Menorca/Minurqa, Girona/Jarunda, Barcelona/Barshaluna, Cordoba/Qurtuba, Gibraltar/Jabal Tarek, or the mountain of Tarek named for the landing point of our general, Galicia/Yilliqiyya, Guadalquivir/Al Wadi al Kabir or the great river.

Though I had arrived in Seville a little lost and uncertain, by the time I left, I felt a kind of peace, without knowing quite where it came from. When I visited the Alhambra, in Granada, many years later, it finally became clear to me: I was moved not just by the splendor of history but by its survival. I took the survival of this history incredibly personally. All these relics reminded me of Damascus, and my beloved childhood home. And I had not been prepared to be so moved as I walked through inner courtyards with Arabic script carved into their walls, not prepared to be so affected by the name of God etched into stone, not just etched but preserved through war, peace, defeat, conquest, and reconquest. It was not only Arab history and heritage that made this so powerful to me but also the blue and green tiles that reminded me of Isfahan, in my grandmother's Iranian homeland. Maybe we are just plain matter and dust, but maybe our stories—or some part of them—our songs, our poetry, the things we preserve with love—live on.

When I ask my brother about Joseph and the stars, he sets me right. According to the Torah, Joseph followed eleven stars out of the wilderness and met the tribe that took him back to his father. Joseph, that beautiful dreamer, was then set upon by his jealous brothers, who tore his robes, a sight so painful for his father to behold that he ripped his own clothing in anguish.

All the signs, the amulets and talismans that follow me, or that I am seeking, have a natural logic and personal clarity that I feel before I understand. I am not surprised when I come across stories and fables of deer—I am supposed to find them. I am certain that there is something about the lives of wolves that I am meant to know even when their appearance is a mystery to me. When I discover Barry

Lopez's ethnography of wolves, I have a calm sense that it has been waiting for me. I don't wonder why it has taken me so long to read his classic work, but I know I came to it at exactly the moment I was supposed to. And the stars, whether Joseph's eleven that guide him home, or the luminescent Sirius, return to me again and again.

The Dog Star was worshipped by the Arab pagans who existed before Islam. They were nomadic tribes, and they used the night star to navigate, to plant their crops, to live and survive. But when the prophet Mohammad (peace be upon him) reveals the Koran to us, there is Sirius, ever present and enfolded there too. A-shira, he is called in the Koran as he is known in Arabic, the mighty star.

As my relationship with the man nears the seven-year mark, my heart is a wasteland, so ravaged and hurt by loss and grief that I need signs that I will survive. I need to know that love is real and pure, and that it redeems us after it breaks us. That it can fight through all wounds, animating and illuminating everything afresh. I know we can be dimmed and dulled by all our feeble hurts and sorrows, but it has never left me that our deer who was abandoned to the Karachi Zoo, Bambi, died of a broken heart. She should have lived, but her heart couldn't take it. I believe my dog Lama died of a broken heart too. And for a period in my life, I think I will also. The deer that materialize before me tell me another ending is possible. I am convinced of this. They are a reminder that love and even grief are explosive material we carry inside us at all times, forever.

The dogs are a part of my personal constellation because I'm lonely. Coco is not just my companion; she is so much more. She is my antidote to loneliness. The wolves, like the deer, survive despite the fact that they are hunted. And the stars, they connect to everything, a reflection of my hungry need to build this celestial body of my own. It surprises and does not surprise me when I learn that the Dog Star's constellation, Canis Major, is made up of four stars besides Sirius, and they all have Arabic names: Adhara, Wezen, Mirzam, and Aludra. They are second-magnitude stars who will likely explode as supernovas—Sirius is the only one who won't. They are, all of them, visible even from light-polluted areas. Scorching, Sirius means in ancient Greek, glowing. My father is burning up there in the sky, he is with me still. I am not alone.

When I adopted Coco, the man and I had been together four years, and he continued to insist that it was too early to discuss having children. Now, even more years later, it was still only me and my dog, though the man remained in the picture, as distant and unyielding as ever. She has kept me sane, made me feel as though I am in a family, has given me the gift of letting me care for something that relies on me to survive. Looking after Coco remains one of my greatest accomplishments in this period when I wandered far from home. I thanked God for Coco, but in my gut, I couldn't help but feel that we were not enough. I tortured myself with longing for more, for a family of my own.

There is a version of this story that is a love story. I have written drafts of that story before abandoning them. I met the man during a dark, strange place in my life, and he helped me through a sea of grief—I was grateful to him, indebted and in love. Yet I was also incredibly vulnerable. I felt I could not speak to anyone about him, and because he understood my fears of abandonment, he held me tight in our secret. I pushed many times to change our relationship, to force it out into the open and encourage some sort of real progress, without which I could never move ahead with my dream of having a child. I never pushed too hard, though, partly because I was victim to the same rotten thinking that plagues so many women: that this would pass, and it would pass because I could change him. I wanted a child so much and I had spent many precious years not having one. It had already been one year, then three, then five, then seven, how much time did the man actually need?

By year seven, this "logic" took on a new, slightly manic overtone. When I had outrun reason, I started to pray, and

I visited shrines and temples on my travels. Allegra and I drove all day one summer in Italy to see the shrine of Saint Rita, saint of impossible causes. I bought crystals, I wore talismans. I took vitamins. One day, Allegra caught me holding a crystal in the small of my palm. "Oh, a gratitude rock," she cooed, "what a good idea." Old me would have guffawed at the idea of a gratitude rock, a term I am embarrassed even to know. But new me was carrying crystals around, so who was I to laugh at anything? If I couldn't convince the man that seven years was a terrible amount of time to make a woman wait to have a baby, then God would persuade him. Or the dynamic power of tourmaline. Or chanting.

By my late thirties, I could think of nothing else. I drove myself crazy with a ragged determination to blame everything except my decision to stay with the man for my failure to have a family. I looked up surahs and listened to Alan Watts and Thich Nhat Hanh. I channeled my frustration into writing. I exercised. I tumbled into a deep depression and stopped eating, seeing people. I lost weight. I started eating again. I injured myself running. I stopped exercising. I stopped eating chocolate, renouncing it as an offering to the universe in exchange for what I wanted, chocolate in exchange for my life's dream. I ran away. I hid. I studied my horoscope. I wrote gratitude lists. At the height of my desperation, at the age of thirty-eight, I called an astrologer a friend swore by. I asked her to do a chart for the whole year, and when she asked me if there was anything in particular I was interested in knowing about, I didn't hedge—will I have a child?

After a week or so, the astrologer sent me a recording and prefaced the year's forecast by gently telling me that she didn't see anything to do with children. Or much else, for that matter. I was running errands while I listened to the recording; by the time she reached March and then April and May, I stopped what I was doing to see if there was something wrong with my ears. There was only stasis to report: *Not much will happen for you in March, well, April also looks quiet . . . May won't be very busy . . . June will be solemn.* And on and on it went till December. It was much later in 2020 when I could think back to this recording and find the humor in it. In January of that year it seemed like the astrologer was broken, seeing nothing, forecasting only silence and solitude. I like to think she forecast the pandemic specifically for me.

I had a nagging, recurring thought: I should just be happy with what I have—this little unit of two, human and dog. We are okay. We need each other, we care for one another. Coco was like a child, in a way, wasn't she? Without me, she could feed herself for an afternoon, tops. But I dismissed this. Somewhere, I insisted to myself, somewhere there is an answer to what my heart desires. I just have to find it. I looked everywhere until eventually, I wondered if I truly was cursed.

Back then, feeling unmoored and uncertain of what I was supposed to do with my one, precious life, in Seville, in what was once known as Ishbiliya, I took a photo of the centuries-old tiles that protect Allah's name. I am not religious, but when I look at it, it gives me succor. It reminds me that I belong somewhere and that somehow, in this place that waits for me, I will be sheltered from my troubles. In a surah named "The Ant," the Koran speaks to us of the deceptions of time and impatience: "Now you see mountains, thinking they are firmly fixed, but they are travelling just like clouds."[22]

Chapter 8

It was the middle of the night in Bali. I was there for a literary festival, jet-lagged, and the man had woken me up with a phone call. Thirty-five had been my deadline, the point at which I imagined I would no longer wait for the man. But there I was, thirty-six, huddled under a mosquito net on the other side of the earth, ever hopeful.

"I am getting older and you are stopping me from having the only thing I've ever truly wanted," I told the man.

"If you're so concerned, why don't you freeze your eggs?"

It was part of his standard response: ignore, fight, and if all else failed, gaslight. The problem wasn't that he was reneging or delaying or wasting my reproductive years, it was that I hadn't taken the time to back up my chances and freeze my eggs. Before this, during an earlier version of this same fight, after I turned thirty-three, the man fobbed me off by asking, somewhat unkindly, why I never stopped bothering him about children. "Do you even know if you can have kids?" he taunted me over the phone. "Have you ever gone to a doctor and checked?" I hadn't, but I made an appointment to do so after that conversation. After my doctor assured me I could have children, I reported the results to the man. "Good"—he shrugged—"then stop rushing me."

But that night, somewhere between dark and light, dusk and dawn in Bali, I took his words in. Friends of mine had suggested this before, some of them had frozen their eggs and told me it had made them feel better, more secure about the future; it had given them some sense of relief. It was starting to become painfully clear to me that if I wanted to be a mother, I didn't have much more time to waste. A week after leaving Bali, I had an appointment in Barcelona to freeze my eggs.

Coco and I booked an Airbnb almost at the far end of the dark sandy beaches of La Barceloneta, in Poblenou. The flat was in a modern loft-style building, everything metal and exposed, and no doors anywhere save the bathroom, but in the evening we could walk five minutes and sit on the beach, away from winter swimmers and volleyball players on a quiet stretch of the windswept shore.

At my first appointment, an Italian doctor with dyed blond hair, her dark roots strong, handed me a bag of syringes and medication. In the waiting room outside, I was the only person sitting alone. Everyone else was in twos, couples, and I noticed a South Asian husband and wife, nervously flicking through a folder and holding hands. I prayed silently that the receptionist would not call me by my full name, but the couple went in before me. I was still there when they reemerged, less nervous, arms around each other, happy and relieved.

I had come at the right time, the doctor said. Ideally, I should have come before thirty-five, but this was the last good year to undertake a freezing. She told me that I could no longer exercise once I started the injections because of something called ovarian torsion—you were unnaturally filling your ovaries up with an abnormal number of eggs and if you ran or jogged or cycled too fast your ovaries could twist, explode the eggs, and kill you. It was rare, the doctor added with tired Italian fatalism, but still, it happened.

"Could I do yoga?"

She folded her hands across her lap. "No."

"Swim?"

"No."

"Lift weights?"

"No."

"Pilates?"

"No."

"You can walk," she offered, "but slowly."

I signed a paper saying I understood the risks and paid for the vials. Before I left, the doctor's assistant showed me by miming where in my stomach I would have to inject myself every night. I was scared, but she handed me a telephone number—the clinic's emergency line, open twenty-four hours a day. "Try to inject yourself at the same time every evening," she said, "and if you have any problems, just call us."

Day One

I was beyond anxious. I had tried to call the man but hadn't been able to reach him since 1:00. It was nearing 7:00, and I was supposed to do my first jab between 7:30 and 8:00. He had been at the movies earlier, but that was hours ago. I called and texted him, no answer. He knew what I was doing and was at pains to show me that he had more pressing matters to attend to, like going to the cinema. I was nervous that I would inject air into my stomach and die painfully. I was worried about getting fat. The doctor had warned me that the body changes dramatically over the course of the hormones and one can feel a little moody. How moody? She described the two weeks of injections as going from normal to three months pregnant, more or less overnight, mood and body wise.

I was worried I'd inject the wrong medicine, worried I'd drop the vial and break it. Even though this is not Karachi and there are no power cuts, I worried that the electricity would get cut. In this nightmare scenario, the fridge would break down and my expensive bag of medicines—which of course I had paid for myself because the man claimed that if women truly believe in equality, *truly truly*, then they will pay for dinners and hotels, expensive birthday presents and fertility treatments for themselves *and* their partners—would be rendered useless. He made sure to practice this philosophy as rigorously as possible. When we were at restaurants and the bill came, he would smile at the waiter and say, "My accountant will take care of that" as he slid the check toward me. The waiters almost never laughed.

He called, finally, before my injection, but we fought and he slammed the phone down. I told him I was scared and didn't want to do this alone. "Don't do it then!" he shouted. Afterward he texted me three times, angry. I thought he might acknowledge that this was hard on me and say something reassuring, or that he would recognize I was in this position only because he didn't have the nerve to tell me the truth, but the last message said simply: "GN." Good night, for when he was sulking and the extra letters would have sounded too friendly.

I decided to walk Coco before doing the injection, delaying until 8:30. Coco trotted around the concrete blocks of Poblenou and did her business quickly. Back in the flat, I held the syringe in my left hand while staring at the time, waiting until exactly half past. I lifted my shirt and jabbed my stomach, pushing the plunger down slowly as my skin filled with something, creating a bubble. There was only Coco to hear my panic, and she watched me with her head cocked to the side, curious. I immediately called the hotline and a kindly voice answered.

"Hello, this is Fatima, IjustdidtheinjectionbutmyskinfilledwithairandIdontknowifIdiditrightandshouldIcometotheclinic?Orgotoahospital?"

Somehow the lady understood me and asked a series of questions before assuring me that it was okay, sometimes that skin-bubble thing happens. "Next time try to inject the other side of your stomach," she said. "And after the needle is in, wait a moment, then dispense the fluid."

"Okay," I answered gratefully. "Thank you."

"Call again if you need," the lady trilled on the phone.

When I put down the phone there was a text from him: "Love u, be careful."

Day Two

I felt okay but as though I was having cramps. I tried to pass the day by entertaining Coco; we took the bus to the other side of Barceloneta, and as we were walking along a more crowded section of the beach, we saw a naked man evaluating the waves before deciding where to dive into them. Coco had to be restrained from leaping in the water after him. Somehow the hours ticked by, yet by the evening, I felt the cramps still building. I called the phone line. Valeria—that was her name—answered once again. "Don't worry," she told me. "It's quite normal to have cramps. Have you done the injection yet?" I hadn't. "Okay, call if you need anything," she said.

When I put the needle in my stomach, something about the syringe plunger didn't work. I panicked and pulled the needle out. I was breathing fast; this injection felt no easier than the day before; it felt worse. I put the needle back in and pressed, and this time it worked and I felt the liquid seep into me. It was surreal. I called Valeria back and she recommended that the next time, I squeeze the part of my stomach that I was about to inject so I had a fleshy target. I thanked her and said good night. I tried to read *The Sound and the Fury* to calm down but hated it. I hated William Faulkner, I hated the characters, and by page 50, my hatred had extended to schoolteachers, the American canon, and everyone on earth who had ever read and/or recommended this book.

Day Three

I left Coco at home to buy groceries and came back to find she'd broken into a ziplock bag and eaten an almond croissant I had been saving for dessert. There was a box of oat cookies nearby, and she'd massacred those too. I was so angry that when she sat on a chair next to mine at the small table in the kitchen in an attempt to make up, I pushed the chair away from me. She hopped off it and crawled under mine. I could feel her staring at me wondering what on earth had happened to me. I was shaking. I felt a thousand things at once: my day was ruined, I was hungry, I was tired, angry, bloated, queasy.

At injection time, I squeezed a roll of my stomach so hard I thought that I should probably release it, but when I did, the needle popped out. I quickly jabbed a new spot and my skin puffed up—worse than the skin bubble the first night. As I was injecting myself with the hormones, the pocket of skin I pinched turned yellow, like decaying fat, and the pores around the injection site enlarged. I felt sick. I called the man and he said, "Put ice on it." Ice was his solution to all medical ailments, from headaches to knee injuries to amputations. I got a cube from the freezer and called the hotline. Valeria answered and sounded perplexed. "Hello, this is Fatima," I began and told her all about the yellow puffiness and the pores. She put me on hold to speak to a nurse. I rubbed the ice on my skin in circles while I waited, my fingertips turning cold. Valeria returned to tell me it was okay, the nurse said I should just massage the spot. "Shouldn't I put ice on it?" I asked as the dwindling cube dripped onto my jeans. "No," she replied, "why would do you something like that? It's not a sports injury."

"Oh, right."

Days Four and Five

He called to tell me that he probably couldn't see me at Christmas. I'd planned this whole fertility exercise to coincide with his schedule, which, until this phone call, included being together over the holidays. In the process of being with the man, I had completely lost myself. That night, with Coco curled up next to me, I wondered: Is this really who I want to have a child with?

I told myself in the dark that this process meant I wouldn't need to depend on him, I wouldn't be in this state of limbo and dependency much longer. Somehow I went back to sleep, but when it was morning and I was in the shower, I found myself in tears. I felt so alone.

Day Six

I called Allegra because I was truly overwhelmed. At the doctor's appointment earlier, they gave me an estimate for the day we could do the egg retrieval. I called the man and asked if he could come. There was silence on the line and then, as though he was talking to a child, he said, "You want me to come and be there for your egg retrieval?"

"Yes please, the doctors said someone has to bring me to the clinic and then take me home and look after me because I will be knocked out. I can't be alone after they do the retrieval. It's two or three days that I have to be careful, and there's Coco, I won't be able to walk her."

"You want me to be there? Me? To walk your dog?" He sounded somewhere between offended and incredulous.

Allegra told me of course she would be there for the procedure, and even though she had an important appointment the day after, she would come a few days before to spend time with me. When Allegra had to leave, our friend Ortensia would come to look after me for the following two days. Another friend, Sophie, told me to write everything down and talked to me often on the phone, making me laugh. Eggxit, we called the process. This made me guffaw every time I said it. I told Allegra that I was struggling with the injections, they'd become painful. "Go to the clinic and have them inject you!" she insisted. "No, they can't." (I'd already asked Valeria this.) "Well, then go to a hospital!" "That's embarrassing," I told her. "Go to a pharmacy," Allegra continued, undeterred. "Pay them something every night and ask them to do it for you."

"No," I sighed, "I can do it. It's not that bad," I promised her. But it was that bad, I just didn't want Allegra to worry.

Day Seven

I felt ill and weepy all the time and my body was swimming with hormones. I did the injections at the Ikea kitchen table because it was where the lighting in the flat was the strongest. The table faced a huge curtainless window that looked out into someone else's living room. Though we were not at eye level, I wondered if the people in the opposite flat could see me, if they felt bad for me injecting my stomach alone every night. Maybe they didn't, but that night I felt bad for me.

Day Eight

I received a text from an old friend of my father who didn't know any of this was going on; it was a random text of kindness. "Your well-being is close to my heart," it said, and when I read it, I wept. I missed my father, I missed being in a family where one's well-being was carried in the hearts of others. I felt weak and tired and regretful, and I tried to remember that I was doing this for myself—but what did that mean? That I was freezing my eggs so I could have a baby alone at some point in the near future? They would freeze the eggs for only five years; was the man really not going to have a child with me within five years? Sitting at my desk, I lit a candle before my injection and then forgot about it until hours later when I noticed the light in the dark.

I am normally responsible and careful. I don't make careless mistakes, I don't leave the gas on, I don't forget my keys, I don't leave candles burning all night long. It rattled me that I could have made such a mistake. Who was I? What was I doing? I didn't recognize myself at all. I couldn't make careless mistakes because there was just me—I was the only one I could rely on, I was the one who had to keep things running smoothly, I couldn't go and burn the house down because there was no one to sound the alarm if I did. Who would have put a fire out? Coco? My arms and legs were shaking, and I felt acutely every wound of all the past years.

For all the time I had known him, I had thought that the man would get better—that he would become kinder, gentler, more like the man I had built him up to be in my head. Because I am stubborn; because I believed him when he was in a good mood; because I thought he was in pain and that's why he was hurtful, controlling, and mean; because I thought that my love would save him, could heal him; and very much because I didn't think someone like me—smart and strong and feisty—could be in an emotionally abusive relationship. But I was. That was the first time I truly realized it. My hands shook. My father's friend's text message had unnerved me because I knew he wanted what was best for me, and I recognized, finally, that the man did not.

Day Nine

Allegra arrived and was instantly a soothing presence. Whatever meanness the man had thrown at me, God had made up for it through Allegra. She was selfless and loving and good and tender. She is the best friend I have ever had and without any doubt, the best human being that I have ever met. She walked Coco with me before and after injection time, and we sat at outdoor cafés at night, as it was still temperate in Barcelona in the winter, and we reclined on metal chairs and had tapas and pretended that we were on vacation and nothing was wrong. She showed me pictures of shoes I might like online and cooked healthy dinners, and we watched TV and laughed in the modern metal flat.

Day Eleven

On the day of the procedure, I was not allowed to eat or drink, and I was terrified that I would forget in the middle of the night and have a sip of water. I repeated, mantra-like, *Do not drink water* so much that the worry seeped into my dreams.

Allegra walked Coco early in the morning while I showered and got dressed; then she took me to the clinic. While the procedure was happening, she went back to the flat to move our things out—I couldn't extend the rental—and then cart everything plus Coco to a new place, a friend's flat on the other side of town that I'd borrowed for the recovery. Allegra had done the emotional labor of ten people in the time I'd known her, never complaining, always cheerful.

In the preoperation room, as I put on the surgical outfit left out for me, a dark navy papery dress that I tied up at the sides, Allegra admired the tailoring. "This is really beautiful, it looks like an Aspesi dress," she exclaimed, trying to distract me from my worries and fears. "You should ask them for another one to take home." I laughed because she was right, and I did ask. A bemused nurse handed me another one, folded neatly.

In the theater, the anesthesiologist asked me if I spoke Spanish. "A little," I said. I was so scared, I was already crying quietly, letting the tears fall down my face. The anesthesiologist pretended she didn't notice. "Can you count to twenty?" Her face was covered by a mask like the ones that soon we would all be wearing as we moved about our lives, but then it was still unfamiliar to us and I wondered if she was smiling underneath it when I told her I'd forgotten how to say the number eight in Spanish. I was laughing because of the anesthesia. It was the last thing I remember.

After the procedure, in the borrowed flat, resting and being looked after by my girlfriends, I told the man how relieved

I was to be done with all the hormone injections. They made me feel dreadful, anxious, and unhappy. I reminded him that the clinic would keep my eggs for only five years. "Oh yeah?" he said. I could hear him tapping on his phone as he spoke to me, doing something else, texting friends, playing chess. "So, what, you can do it again in five years?"

One of the many things the man taught me was how to run. He was athletic, an elegant runner with impressive endurance, never tiring, never collapsing in a messy heap. Nothing broke him during his runs, not exhaustion, not time—which he didn't believe in anyway—or pain or discomfort. He could run in sneakers or barefoot, it didn't matter. This was what made him unusually excellent at most things he chose to do—his stamina, fortitude, but most of all his patience. When he was determined about something, he was tenacious.

Before the man, I had been a lifelong abstainer from exercise. I dabbled in yoga for my anxiety and swam in the summer but never had a real exercise regime. Again, here, the man had been right when he decided I should take up jogging. I loved it. Running was meditative. I loved the silence in my head when I ran and the feeling of euphoria as my body overtook my restless mind. It charged me with an energy and happiness that coursed through me for the rest of the day. Anytime I was anxious or worried, I put on my shoes and went for a run. It transformed my life, and like many runners before me, I became obsessed. And, as with any obsession, I injured myself overdoing it.

But the man knew how to cure that too so I could keep going without having to forsake my new fixation. The key was you had to find the right shoes—only Asics would do—and once you had them, you had to work on your gait. You must never land on your heel and always keep your arms lightly bent by your sides, not flailing about. The slower you ran, the longer you could go; this was important. The man would nod approvingly at joggers he encountered on the street. "Good stance," he would mumble, "excellent runner." He gave me books on running and sent me YouTube videos on other such perfect joggers to study so that I would get better and better.

"When you struggle and you think you can't keep going, remember it's all in your mind," he told me. "You can trick your mind. You can trick it to do anything."

I was a slow runner, just as instructed, but after a couple of miles, I tired. I wasn't made for long distance, but the man dismissed my concerns. "You trick your mind like this," he told me, letting me in on his secrets. "You tell yourself, I'll run to that tree over there and then I'll stop. But when you get to that tree, you erase the thought and start again: no, I'll run to that lamppost farther away. Then I'll stop. And you point farther and farther away, erasing as you go."

He did that with me too, all the time stretching my boundaries and limits until he had pushed them so far I could no longer see my stopping point. Do egg freezing a second time? I didn't even want to do it the first time. I thought that when I hit thirty-six, I would leave him. That was my signpost, just as thirty and thirty-three and thirty-five had been. And now here I was, wondering if forty was too late a signpost. With his cold, almost sinister, patience, the man was capable of keeping me on ice forever. For a long while I thought it was my fault, that I wasn't thinking hard enough about how to solve this deadlock or that I had some quality, some defect, that rather than lighting his urgency only delayed him.

Chapter 9

And then the man hit Coco. I wish I could say I left the man immediately, but I didn't. I stayed. This, then, is a record of a mistake I will never make again.

It was five months after Coco's bad pregnancy. I was thirty-eight. Allegra and I didn't know what to call it, lurching between "bad pregnancy," "the awful thing," "that time," "the incident"—very similar to how the man, it occurs to me, referred to our relationship—"the situation." Coco recovered from the pain and confusion of her loss slowly. The young vet who told me I mustn't give her my hand because she would confuse it for a puppy also told me I mustn't, under any circumstances, give her a toy as a baby replacement. But what did he know? He couldn't even tell that she was carrying one wildly deformed pup, not two. I ignored him and bought her a long toy snake, its slithery body stuffed with foil so that it rustled when you coiled it up. Its soft fur was an indigo blue, and for a while, Coco carried the snake everywhere, pulling it—it was five times longer than she was—up and down stairs, reaching for it to sleep with when she sat at my feet as I worked, and dragging it around the house with her on her rounds.

Eventually she let me take it away and we returned to our normal life. The snake was not a baby, just a plaything she sometimes, but not always, wanted. Allegra and I tried not to talk about "the incident," and I resolved to get Coco spayed. That summer, she started to have strange fits, seizures that would paralyze her for a minute or two, freezing her limbs in contracted positions, rendering her unable to walk or move. The first time it happened, we had just returned home from a walk and I sat on the floor and held my frozen dog, stroking her with one hand and calling the vet with the other. But then the fit ended and she shook herself off and started walking normally, seemingly undisturbed by the sudden attack.

It was the first summer of the pandemic, and I had waited most of the year to see the man. He couldn't and then wouldn't travel in the initial months of Covid after being badly struck by the virus. I wanted an end to our impasse. I needed to move on with my life, and if it wasn't going to be with him, then I wanted to say goodbye. Not that things are ever so clean; I knew they wouldn't be this time either. I'd said goodbye to him so many times before.

One evening, when Coco was in heat, her first season since "the thing" had happened, Allegra and I were walking in a small park when a handsome Jack Russell, all white with a little smudge of brown around one eye and a bull's-eye on his back, came bounding up to us. Just that morning the vet had told me we could sterilize Coco a few weeks after her season was finished. "But be careful with her over the next few days," Coco's vet, Jesus, warned, "if you don't want her to get pregnant again. These are the dangerous days." I laughed out loud. "Don't worry Doctor, I'm not putting myself through that again." The vet laughed along. "Good to hear it," he said.

That evening, the Jack Russell and Coco danced around each other, both of their tails wagging madly, Coco's high in the air. I tried to take her away from him, calling her name and attempting to hold her harness, but she was so happy, flirting away, that I didn't have the heart to insist. Who was I to stand in the way of nature? The boy's owner and I watched our dogs leaping and playing. "She's in heat," I told him. "Is your dog fixed?" He wasn't, and his owner had always wanted him to have a puppy. I nodded, taking in the information. My arms were folded across my chest. "If we had puppies, would you take one?" I asked cautiously. He definitely would. "Look," I bargained, "let's meet again tomorrow and if it happens it happens. If it doesn't, it doesn't." If this was the detached approach to dog romance, then I was a high lama. I had no expectation, no desire.

The next evening, I took Coco back to the park and the two mated almost immediately, I and the other dog's human sitting beside them, awkwardly trying to make conversation over the whining and barking and belabored panting. Coco acted characteristically dramatic as soon as it was over, scrambling like a cartoon character, her nails kicking up clouds of dirt, in her desperation to get away as fast as possible.

She vomited through the next night, big puddles of chewed-up rice and dog food. Coco ran out of my room and into Allegra's to wake her up and show her the vomit. She whined gently like she does when she wants to go out, and Allegra took her out to the street, where she threw up again and again.

Two weeks later, she was mostly her old self, snoozing next to me in the mornings and turning her nose up at every bowl of food I offered her at mealtimes. Exasperated by her refusal to eat, I walked to a supermarket and bought slices of deli chicken. She ate them only when fed by hand but ignored the pale slices of meat if I placed them on a plate for her.

When the man finally arranged for us to have some time together, "Bring Coco" was all he asked of me. He still wanted only trips to new destinations, anonymous places where neither of us had neighbors or friends or daily routines. This way, there was no risk of the two of us seeing what an actual life together might be like.

I arrived early in Florence and checked in at the hotel to get a few hours of sleep before he arrived. By noon, Coco and I had woken up and there was no sign of him, no messages, no calls. I estimated his arrival like a detective might search a crime scene scrubbed of all evidence and clues—by using instinct and guessing. I checked airport arrivals pages, but I never knew where he was traveling from, as he traveled so much for work, or on what leg of his journey my visit was, so I simply waited. It was colder than I thought it would be in late September, and after sitting still in the hotel room all day, Coco and I went out to buy a hat. When we came back, we saw him in the lobby.

I could see the agitation in his body before he even turned around. He knew that I had come to meet him expecting an answer: Do we move forward, or do we end things? I moved to embrace him, it had been many months since we met, but he pulled away from me sharply and bent down to pet Coco. He spoke to her in a soft, sweet voice, picking her up and kissing her ears, which stood erect and alert.

I was used to these cold touches, they tended to last a day or two, and then he'd relax. This time, however, he remained distracted and stony. One night, we went to dinner, Coco strutting along on the lead, and as soon as we sat down, I was struck by debilitating stomach cramps. I hunched over in my chair and tried to drink a warm tea, but the pain was so piercing I could barely sit. This has happened to me off and on since I was a child, a stress response, my body's way of telling me it can't take any more of whatever I am putting it through. I stood up to go back to the hotel, telling him I would meet him there later. "I'll come with you," he said, his annoyance only thinly disguised. Our food had just arrived. I didn't want to have a fight. "Honestly, I'm fine, I deal with these all the time," I told him, meaning it and wanting to be alone. "You eat, I'll see you later." I lived alone, I knew how to take care of myself. And I didn't have the energy to deal with another one of his moods.

But he came with me and made me a makeshift hot water bottle with an old plastic water bottle wrapped in a sweater. It helped. But I could see he was an unhappy caregiver, his forehead lined with the marks of what was becoming a permanent frown. "Thank you," I whimpered. He nodded in return, his tenderness reserved for Coco, whom he stroked and cuddled and spoke to in that sweet voice. I slept with the bottle pressed to my stomach. Coco eventually huddled up next to me and fell asleep.

The next afternoon, my stomach was better, and after a late morning breakfast and brisk dog walk, we returned to the hotel. I was putting away more dog food that Coco had refused to eat, tucking a plate into the tiny mini fridge. The man was on the unmade bed with Coco, chucking her left and right and pretending his hand was a pincer coming to bite her, when Coco snapped at him. Snarling, she bared her teeth and threatened him with a bite. I don't know if she nipped at him or not, but she was angry, and before I knew what had happened, he stood up and smacked her with an open hand.

"What are you doing?" I shouted, shocked, trying to understand what had happened.

"She attacked me." His voice was loud and ragged; he spat out the words.

Coco was cowering, submissive, her ears folded flat against the back of her head.

"You don't hit her." I felt sick. "She could be pregnant; she could be protecting herself."

"You're going to let your dog bite me?"

"You're too rough with her."

I picked her up in my arms and held her to my chest. So many thoughts rushed through my head: was she hurt, what if she lost another litter, what if this fear stayed with her forever, what kind of grown man can hit a small Jack Russell? It took me a moment to realize that I was shaking too.

"I will discipline her if she misbehaves with me."

"No, you won't. She's my dog, and if she needs disciplining, I will do it."

"She's my dog too."

No. No she wasn't. He never looked after her, never stayed with her at night, sleeping on the floor next to her because she was ill, never spent hours walking around the park to give her exercise, never paid a single vet's bill, never went searching for her favorite dog food when she was being a fussy eater, never cooked her rice when her stomach was bad, never canceled a plan because he couldn't find anyone to watch her, never cleaned up her vomit, and had consistently refused to pick up her poo, which was—as an antimaterialist Buddhist—beneath him. He had never done anything except enjoy what dogs give so freely: her love.

"Don't touch my dog."

I don't remember what he said next. I only remember what I kept saying, again and again, as I put on her harness and grabbed my bag and her leash. "Don't touch my dog."

Chapter 10

At my most fragile and vulnerable, desperately scared about the path ahead, I develop a new psychosis: I trawl dog shelter websites and accounts and write email after email with an energy that I haven't had in months, years even:

Hello! How are you? I have a Jack Russell and I'm looking to adopt. I'd like a female (or a male!) who is a puppy and so they can grow up with Coco (or maybe an older dog, a senior). I'm looking for a dog who is a small size (actually, big size is ok too! Or medium?) and who is good on the leash *but can walk without one too*, a dog I can train or who is trained and is looking for a good home! Thank you! Ps I can also volunteer? Or foster?

I am not going to count how many notes like this I send to shelters all over the world. I fall in love with every sad story I read, mentally rename the dog, start organizing for their arrival, and then receive an email back saying they have already been adopted in Athens or Lebanon or wherever. I want a new life, a real life, with roots and family. And if I have to make that family myself and it has to be unconventional, then I will do it. I am done relying on others. I am tired of waiting for my life to miraculously change, I will change it, and I will do so in the way that I know best. I will adopt a dog on whom I can lavish all this manic energy. I am undeterred. I write letters faster, fill out adoption forms, and send DMs on Instagram. I get answers but somehow never an actual dog.

"Is what you really need in life right now an abused German shepherd?" one friend asks.

"Yes! It is!"

"Don't you think it will be hard to travel with a beagle with an adrenal problem?" another friend wonders.

"No, it's fine, we're not even traveling anymore thanks to Covid!"

"Won't Coco be terribly upset when the galgo with three legs turns up?"

"She already has a terrible personality, who'll be able to tell!"

I have an answer for everything. It's the most enthusiastic I've been in a long time, though I start to suspect my name is on some sort of international shelter DNR list.

When a shelter that hasn't heard about me yet writes back and continues the process for adopting whatever dog I've inquired about, I panic and back off. I get quite far in the process, however. The shelter calls me, and we have a long conversation, me pointing out all my red flags in what I consider an act of radical transparency:

I travel a lot,
my dog cannot stand other dogs,
she is possessive,
has she ever lived with another dog? No, haha, she would hate that.

But inexplicably, the shelter schedules a home visit. I am certain I will fail the visit, how can I not when Coco launches at the shelter lady and barks at her nonstop for over an hour? But I pass. I get an email that defies logic, letting me know that I'm approved to adopt and my new dog, a German shepherd, can be picked up in two weeks' time.

For a week I mull this over and mentally plan for our new arrival, even buying a big bone along with a small one for Coco and loading up on extra dog treats. But then I feel a cold dread creep over me. How will I travel with a massive dog? What if Coco hates her—more than likely, guaranteed—and what if the shepherd attacks Coco? How will I ever leave them alone together? I'll never be able to leave the flat, not even to go to the post office? I call the shelter and tell them I am nervous for Coco, and she will need some kind of training to be able to accept another dog in our lives before I can adopt. I apologize profusely. I feel terrible, I feel like a commitment phobe, like someone who wants to reap the myriad benefits of having a dog—the love, the companionship, the warmth—but none of the responsibility.

I feel like the man.

As lousy as I feel about reneging on the poor German shepherd, I keep writing to shelters. I am a bit more careful, simultaneously trying to make super-clear how inappropriate I am as a candidate and how well meaning my intentions are, offering all kinds of in-between solutions instead of adopting: donating, sending care packages of dog food and blankets, fostering, putting friends in touch with the shelters, posting about their dogs. I do this for a good four years. I make friends with some of the (mostly) women who run these shelters around the world, though understandably, others want nothing to do with me after having wasted hours of their time already.

During this time, I am saved by people who materialize out of thin air exactly when I need them. My best friend from college and I talk, and I tell him all the things I have kept quiet. We had lost each other to different lives and struggles and changes and, in the process, lost years of our friendship. When we put down our phones, he sends me a message: Let's promise we'll never lose touch again. We swear, and I realize that I still believe in promises.

My girlfriends take turns coming to visit me so I'm not alone alone. One day, two friends take me to a forest I had no idea existed so we can hike with our dogs, and I am flooded with a joy I had forgotten I was capable of. We walk on the raw, rough earth, stepping on twigs, while the dogs leap over weak, cold streams of fresh water. It drizzles a soft patter of rain and I am reminded of wonder.

In spite of these brief respites from constant sadness, eventually, I crash. And this is the worst I have felt in a long time. I wake up tired after having slept through the night; I lose so much weight I don't fit into any of my clothes anymore; every task, no matter how small or uplifting, becomes impossible. I can't write, I can't read, my only sanctuaries are gone. I am drowning, and for the first time in my life, maybe because I am older or maybe because I have spent all my reserves of strength, I finally accept defeat. There is no happy ending, no miracle, no hopeful possibilities for the future. Maybe this is what my life is supposed to be. I try to remember my father, to remember how incredibly lucky I am, but it is hard to see this through the sadness that falls over me and simply cannot be lifted.

At this point, when I am stressed enough to have forgotten the kindness of the world, things happen that make me feel something powerful. It's a morning when everything has gone wrong: I have a repairman over fixing a busted freezer, another coming to fix a leaking shower, Coco barking like mad at one of her many enemies down the road (at last count she has three major enemies, all at least twenty-four pounds bigger than she is), and I am too tired to make something for lunch. When the deliveryman arrives, I go downstairs, frazzled and hungry, my eyes red and puffy. He gets off his bike; I can see from his face that we come from the same country, both strangers living in a new land. He riffles through his bag; there are several orders from the restaurant I have ordered from. He gives me my order, and I pause for a second to confirm it's mine; it is, and I reach out my hand to give him a tip, but either I do this too slowly or he is newer than I am in this country, and for a second, I can see a shadow of confusion pass over his face. Then he reaches out his hand warmly and innocently, almost as if to hold mine, to squeeze it, correcting his movement seamlessly when he notices the tip. I am so moved by this instinct we have that transcends everything, every possible barrier, to connect. Whatever our circumstances and whatever those around us, we are built to respond to kindness, to warmth.

"Everything is a miracle when you are alive," the poet Omar Sakr has written, "I am learning that against my will."[23] On Ashura, the tenth day of Muharram, the mourn-ing period for Shiite Muslims as they remember Imam Hus-sain and his family killed in Karbala, it is tradition to give food and water to the hungry and thirsty. Imam Hussain and his family were encircled in the desert, seventy-two people surrounded by four thousand soldiers, who cut them off from food and water. When Imam Hussain approached the soldiers to beg for water for his infant son, parched and desperate, they killed the infant in the arms of his father. My brother sends me a video from the *sabeel* that we always organize outside our house. He is wearing black and sit-ting on the street, washing the dishes. He is barefoot. He reminds me of our father.

On a short trip to Madrid, I walk alone in the Prado, a museum I love, and stand in front of the Goya painting of the drowning dog. That is enough. Outside the museum, a man plays a saxophone with absolutely no rhythm at all. He is just making loud, clanging noise, irritating passersby, who curse under their breaths and shake their heads. But the fat yellow Labrador busking with him, wailing along to his owner's music, is so adorable that it is also enough. A song is enough, a scent is enough—twice when I am walking Coco I catch a whiff of my father's cologne in the middle of nowhere; I am so shocked and happy that I doubt it is real and stop in the street to smell my hands, even the poo bags in my pocket in case they have been perfumed with Geoffrey Beene's Grey Flannel since the last time I bought them, but it's not the bags and it's not my hands, it's my father's cologne, floating around me in the air. There are signs everywhere that life is pure and good, even as we struggle to stand in the world. Even as the body keeps score of all our wounds, and our hearts are heavy with pain, what a miraculous thing it is to survive.

I write this down because I want to say that there is something greater than grief, something more ferocious and tenacious. Because I clung to my dog for a good reason, because I tried, because I fought for love, though it didn't work. This explains some part of the alchemy of what Coco means to me. Not all of it, but some. There is something celestial about dogs—what they teach us about love and time and the smallness of our own beings and place in the world. Perhaps this is true of all animals, of all living beings, but there is no other animal with whom we are so intimately intertwined—one that lives with us, depends on us for not just food but attention and care, that guards us and adores us regardless of our failings. Most people I know who have cats begrudgingly acknowledge that they are often unsure if their cats actually like them. Not dogs: they love us at our worst and in doing so, remind us that love, in whatever form we find it, truly does redeem us.

And my little dog, who came into my life just as a part of it was breaking down, accompanied me through the narrow years of my adult life, all while teaching me new ways to love and be loved. She was there beside me when the free life I had made for myself, rather than the one I had inherited, was dismantling too, and with her presence she offered me comfort and hope. At the time, I thought these were small lessons. But back then, I didn't think there was all that much we could learn from animals either.

Chapter 11

"I'm sorry to tell you, but it's an invasion," Allegra warns ominously.

It is autumn and we are entering our second lockdown of 2020. Allegra and I are at her family home in Tuscany. We have come to this house, tucked away in a forest, ostensibly for a small break, two weeks at most, for a bit of sunshine and so Coco can run around in the wild. But now we are stuck here as Italy imposes another lockdown. We made a pact, after the good luck of getting stuck together in Oxfordshire, that we wouldn't face another lockdown alone. We are the only ones of our circle of friends who aren't married, don't have kids, or aren't in the middle of divorces. She has been a godsend to me in these lonely years, offering me not just shelter but laughter and happiness and solace. One birthday, she wraps small gifts for me—a key chain, a whistle for dogs, a coin purse—which she announces as being from my father and grandmother and gives them to me over the course of the day. She is as effusive as I am guarded and tight-lipped, telling me how proud she is of me whenever I do the most minor thing, like helping her with her computer updates (she sees any computer knowledge, no matter how basic, as a sign of genius). She takes me to look at makeup or clothes, and her enthusiasm makes it possible to believe that if I buy this one concealer, I will not only correct my dark under-eye circles but also defeat time itself. Allegra is like an older and younger sister all at once; she makes me laugh no matter how gloomy I feel and talks to me in made-up accents, reminding me of my father, a great mimic and mood uplifter himself. How did I get so lucky to have a friend like her?

We have known each other long enough that I can forbid Allegra from speaking to me until noon, when I have had enough coffee, worked, and am fit for human interaction. And every day she forgets and bursts into my room telling me the twenty things she's thought of since waking up five minutes before. I glare at her as she barrels away, rapid fire, smiling a huge smile, each story interrupting the preceding one midway. She is decent enough not to remind me that I am in fact in her house while I am imposing this rule on her.

We thought it would do Coco good to be out in nature after this *annus horribilis.* There are deer in the nearby forest, though one doesn't see them often, as well as foxes, birds, wild boars, and more. And now, Allegra informs me, we have been invaded by bugs. She holds up a *Halyomorpha halys*, otherwise known as a brown marmorated stinkbug. She's correct, these winged monsters are everywhere. This one is wrapped in a kitchen towel to protect against the smell, but so odorous is this tiny insect, its rancid scent radiates through the fabric and settles on your fingers anyway. Their bodily fluid is toxic, and touching them, hurting them, killing them, even just looking at them sideways, triggers their foul odor. Various scientific articles say they smell like cilantro. Reader: they do not smell like cilantro. They smell like the putrid fumes of an old, unwashed car that's been set on fire after being filled with decaying garbage.

The bugs are "marmorated" because their shells are marbled, veined, a greenish brown, patterned like the skin of a python. Except a python infestation would have been preferable. These stinkbugs are small and resilient, they thrive in hot environments but do just fine in the cold, and they eat over 250 species of plants—this makes them "versatile," according to scientists. Pesticides do almost no damage to them, their six long legs allow them to hover over food, and they can drill into and eat from the insides of plants and vegetables, avoiding chemical-laden exteriors entirely. One type of pesticide, the pyrethroid variety used in the United States, was thought to work on them until a day or so after its use, "when more than a third of the ostensibly dead bugs rose up, Lazarus-like and calmly resumed the business of demolition."[24] In plain English, they are indestructible.

When I come out of the shower, there's one in my towel. At breakfast, one drops into my coffee. They hide in the corners of the windows, in shoes, socks, under the arms of chairs, on sofa cushions, over doorframes. They lurk in light fixtures and inside lampshades, and they fly drunkenly, loudly, onto our pillows at night. We can always hear them: their noisy buzzing is followed by a second of silence and then, the dreaded click they make upon landing.

After they've got used to us, they come right at us, aiming for our faces and hair. They plop down next to Coco as she naps on a chair, they hide in oven mitts, in saucepans, under desks, over desks, inside desk drawers. They're not terribly impressive fliers, managing a mile and a half a day on average, often flying headfirst into walls. They have been described as "graceless and impossibly dumb" (a journalist) but also "magnificent and dastardly" (an entomologist)—both of these are accurate and yet neither description paints the full picture of horror these creatures deserve.[25]

By the start of October, Coco is pregnant again, and this time around, everything is different. Her tummy swells and her teats enlarge. She looks like a cello—slim on top, with a heavy middle and bottom. Soon, she can no longer jump from the floor into my arms. She grunts when she flops off a chair and has to be airlifted back into it. Allegra doesn't know any vets nearby, but a pair of holistic ones are recommended to us. They prove to be exactly what they sound like: they refuse to do an X-ray because of the negative effect of magnetic vibrations. I almost regret insisting because they clearly have no idea how to use such advanced technology, telling me first that there are no puppies, then that they're dead in utero, before deciding that "no, hang on, sorry, they're alive. And, oh, look, there are four puppies." But we don't know any other vets, so I begrudgingly make a follow-up appointment.

By the end of the month, winter has announced itself with a cool blue mist in the early mornings. I take Coco on walks through the forest nearby. She waddles, nose close to the earth, barking at the squirrels and birds with abandon. In the daytime it is still warm, and we both tire as we climb the rolling trails. One day I see a fox as she spots Coco and quickly hides. I don't alert Coco; our walks already take double the time they ought to, with Coco stopping to pee every two yards, announcing herself to this kingdom of strangers. The first time Coco ever saw a deer was in this forest. She howled, throwing her head back and wailing with excitement. When we walk in the wild now, we are quiet, careful not to frighten them away. But though the deer don't appear, even Coco abides by this pact, this silence between us and the wild.

I don't know what goes through her mind when she carries twigs and pebbles in her mouth as though foraging and saving for the winter, which she only started doing in the pregnancy. In the dark, near a thicket of bamboo trees that form a hidden sanctuary, the air noticeably cooler, we hear animals that sound like macaques shrieking and screaming, though I know there can't be monkeys here, in rainy northern Italy. Up in the forest, there is a terrace of olive trees, and as the season changes, the olives are harvested, taken to be pressed into oil, leaving a carpet of bitter black beads strewn all over the ground. One day, a falcon glides above us as we walk. Coco and I both stop to watch its passage, she with her head cocked, tracking the falcon's shadow on the ground, which looks as though the bird's wings are pulling through the trees, dappled with evening light. Before, I would have worried the falcon would snap her up, my delicate dog. But now I don't worry; she's much too fat to carry.

My loneliness is taking a strange form. I am used to a high concentration of isolation, working long hours with no one to speak to or see, but that is a choice, a discipline. I miss the world too much to live like this, afraid of breath and air. Women my age were constantly told to focus on our careers, and promised as we were growing up and studying that we would have plenty of time for families and children. Gen X, the generation before us, was told they could have it all, but that, like most assurances, turned out to be a lie. Besides, I always thought a biological clock was a trope of the patriarchy, used to control women, that it was as real as the boring and crude clichés of women's intuition or premenstrual moodiness. But I am wrong. Even if Coco were not expecting another litter, even if I were not thirty-eight, this gnawing hunger has come to define my nights and days. The longing I have for children is a longing I carry everywhere. And it makes me feel all the more alone. The new kind of loneliness introduced by the pandemic comes with a continual trimming of life for us all, as so many of us ask when we will be able to go home, and how we will be able to do all the things we thought we had endless time to do. When will we feel less heartbroken, less hurt?

Barry Lopez tells us there were no stories of lone wolves for Native Americans. Wolves were always of a pack. I have lived so long under the assumption that I was a solitary animal that it breaks me now, in the quiet of this interminable pandemic, to understand that I am not. "The strength of the pack is the wolf, the strength of the wolf is the pack," Kipling wrote in *The Second Jungle Book*. "The wolf that keeps the law will prosper. The wolf that breaks it must die."[26]

*   *   *

A dog can deliver at any point between fifty-six and seventy-two days after conception, and as Coco and I near the second month, the pups start to squirm and jostle in her belly, creating visible ripples underneath her skin. The puppies seem to be punching, turning, twisting, and poking, all in unison. I remember being seven years old and placing a palm on my aunt's stomach when she was pregnant with my cousin and feeling her taut skin jump with every kick. Coco doesn't seem to be bothered by the feverish action going on inside her; at most she glances at her stomach with indifference as her puppies kick away. When she sits on my lap, I feel ticklish, as though there are ants crawling all over me. Coco ignores the moving puppies and naps, huffing as she plops left and right until she is comfortable, on her back, legs in the air like an overturned piano.

Allegra and I plan the weeks ahead gingerly, cautiously. I order all the whelping material again and reread the same books I hid after the spring. When a friend's ex-husband tells me he knows the best vet in the region, I jump at the offer of an introduction. He was not lying. Dr. Stefano, whose face I will never see fully as it's always hidden away behind his mask, is a confident, accomplished vet. He knows how to use an X-ray machine, doesn't offer me homeopathic medicine to cleanse Coco's aura of bad vibes, and reassures me—"Don't worry," he says, "this appears to be a healthy pregnancy. Coco will be fine."

On a Sunday evening, just after day fifty-six of her pregnancy, Coco goes into labor in her whelping bed in my room. She bites her bedding in pain, which is the only thing that is the same as last time. I find it miraculous that animals deliver litters by themselves, guided only by a primal knowledge. By 11:53 p.m., the first puppy is born, a girl, all white with a black nose. Coco breaks the amniotic sac around the puppy and severs the umbilical cord with her teeth before cleaning her. The next follows soon after, a boy. When I try to move her firstborn, worried that she will be trampled as her mother, responding to advancing contraction pain, stomps and twirls in her bed, in one swift movement Coco halts her biting and her digging and tucks the wet white pup under her chin, her eyes locked on mine. She holds the puppy to her neck, not breaking my gaze. I understand and pull my hand away. She is a mother now, the child is hers, not mine.

Until this moment, until approximately 12:23 a.m., I had been the sun, the moon, and the stars for Coco. And she my trusted lieutenant. But now the order of the universe has been altered. By 3:00 a.m., they are all here. There are five of them. Three girls and two boys, tiny suckling creatures, blind and deaf, but, guided by their mother's smell and touch, they attach to her and feed.

*   *   *

The first week or two after the puppies are born, I don't sleep. I still haven't left the man. But I am determined to do so. Especially now, after the arrival of Coco's babies. I no longer trust him, and every time I think of the moment he struck her, I am filled with anger at him, and shame at myself. My eggs, successfully extracted, are in a freezer in Barcelona. Nothing came of the process. While I am in Italy, the clinic sends me their yearly reminder asking what I would like to do: destroy the eggs or preserve them another year? I print their email out, circle "preserve," sign the paper, and send it back to them. Whatever relief Eggxit had given me at the time has dissipated; now it is simply more bureaucracy I must contend with, along with visas and article pitches and bills.

Witnessing the care that Coco, a lifelong grouch, lavishes on her young, I suspect that I am having some sort of breakdown. When the man calls me, I slam the phone down on him and refuse his calls. I go weeks without any desire to contact him. I put pillows on the floor to be close to Coco, so I can feed her and watch over her in the middle of the night. I sweep up stinkbugs, trapping them in tissue paper before they buzz and land near the puppies, energetically flushing them down the toilet—the only means we have found to dispose of them.

Allegra and I operate in shifts, taking Coco out for walks, bringing her plates of ground-up meat and bowls of water. From not letting me touch the puppies, now Coco cries when one of them has squirmed too far from her body, whimpering for my attention. When I come to her, she stares at the stray puppy and back at me until I understand. I am desperate to touch them, these little pink things that look like rodents, their round, minuscule ears still flat against their heads, eyes squeezed shut. When they suckle, they paw at their mother's stomach, pushing their heads back and stretching their arms out against her skin as they feed noisily. They kick the firstborn, the smallest, off whatever teat she's on, elbowing her every chance they get. Again and again, I reattach her next to the bigger pups headbanging away at the feed.

We cannot get an appointment with Dr. Stefano the morning after the birth, and I know Coco needs calcium now that she is feeding her babies. We call the holistic vets, who are over in a flash. "No, no," Lady "Olistico" says, "you don't need calcium."

"But the books say?"

"Well, you can have this tincture of St. John's wort and dandelion, which will be very healing for Coco."

"Thanks, but I'd prefer the calcium prescription."

"It's really unnecessary," the lady olistico says, at which point I am telepathically trying to tell Allegra to remove her from the room before I bite her. Allegra's eyes dart nervously between us. The lady olistico steps away from Coco, who is growling at her (she never growls at Dr. Stefano) and mixes a liquid in the corridor. She scribbles something on a piece of paper, and I, sleep deprived, imagine it's a prescription for the calcium that EVERY VET ON EARTH recommends for a newly nursing dog. But when I look at the paper the olistico has handed me, it says:

> Star of Bethlehem,
> Elm,
> Splifix,
> Crab apple.

Between clenched teeth I tell Allegra—who would be nice to a burglar if she caught him in the middle of robbing her house, even pointing out high-value items he might have missed—that my sense of humor is close to failing. She calls Dr. Stefano one more time, and we drive all over town in the rain to pick up the calcium prescription.

Chapter 12

ngmar Bergman's 1968 film *Hour of the Wolf* is about an artist who has a breakdown while on a secluded island with his wife. It takes place mostly between midnight and dawn. In the hours when people are supposed to lay down their worries for rest, Bergman's artist hallucinates and goes slowly mad. Bergman calls this time in the dark of the night the "hours of the wolf"; it is "when most people die, when sleep is the deepest, when nightmares are more real. It is when the sleepless are haunted by their deepest fear, when ghosts and demons are most powerful."[27] The Hour of the Wolf is also the hour when most children are born, Bergman says. I think about this at night, lying in the sleepless dark. I was born during the hours of the wolf. I don't know when exactly, there is no one I can ask.

I spend my wolf hours listening to the forest. The time falls easily into morning. Like most cyclical insomniacs, I'm terrorized by the idea of insomnia's return. I won't listen to stories about insomnia, try to avoid reading about it, and when asked will always share the little tricks that helped me. I say little because against a gnawing, ferocious sleeplessness, what power do we truly have? No matter your body's drooping helplessness, your eyes refuse to close. You lie awake listening to the quiet, then the birds, then the cars, then people speaking and realize you've lost the entire night. Your forgone sleep claws at you like an itch, making you angry and aggressive all day. You can't nap or else you won't sleep again at night. You can't work because you haven't slept, and every word said to you is an assault on your poor, tired mind. I've blocked out those nights for years, nearly a decade, but now, just like that, they're back.

The birds whistle and caw, one night a bird—an owl? I wonder—trills loopy music. At first, I think it whimsical and sweet, but as the night wears thin it sounds different—jagged and frightened. Birds sing in dialects, like humans they have regional accents. The owl whose music is alternately beautiful and haunting is, I decide, just singing in Italian. Another night, I hear through my window a pack of boars, a sounder, carousing through the dark wilderness. I can hear them running, squealing, and tearing down the unlit paths. Sounders are usually made up of mothers and their young, and together, they do serious damage. Rooting up soil with their tusks, eating crops, destroying growth. Other nights, the music is in the quiet that blankets the forest before a storm. When the storm comes, everything howls. But before, there is nothing, not even a rustling sound.

One day earlier in the summer, I saw a man in the park lying in the grass, his baby stretched across his chest. They were laughing. The father lifted his head and smiled brightly at his child, and the child, eyes wide, tilted his small head as far as it would go and howled with delight. When the man sat up from the grass, as he and his family packed their things, I saw his face for a moment. He was not handsome. But he was beautiful, he was happy.

One evening, I am standing in front of a glass door, lost in my thoughts and watching for the deer. It is their hour, the changing of the light, eventide. But they are nowhere, there is only the orange of burning sunlight setting into the sky.

Coco appears out of the blue beside me, the fur on her neck raised and her spine curved, and she starts to snarl, baring her teeth. I look out into the forest, but I can't see anything in the glowing twilight. Just as I wonder what she is threatened by, a cascade of flesh and hair twirling almost midair materializes from the ether. Three enormous dogs race past the door. They come like ghosts, apparitions, so

fast you see them almost in slow motion. They are playing and running and jumping. They are silent, I never hear
them, only see them. They are gone in seconds. Allegra is
nearby, and she sees the wild dogs as happy and friendly, but
I am unnerved. "They were almost at our door!" I tell her.
I saw them as danger. What if they had hurt Coco? What
if the puppies had been outside? The wild dogs glided by
the thin puppy fence we had just put in the garden like
ballerinas, limbs outstretched, grazing all our borders: door,
chicken wire, doorstep. I don't care about the wild at that
moment; I don't care about free or native animals. I am lit
by trespass then. I care at that moment only about property:
mine.

Though he is still in the picture, in my mind, the man
had disappeared. The puppies had taken me away from a
painful relationship the way nothing else could—not my
own dignity, logic, or any knowledge of my own. I want to
have a child. I want to be alone. I want to be loved but not
known. But only if I am known, truly known, can it be love.

On the tenth night, Coco starts to bury the pups. By then
I have begun to relax my vigil, going down to the kitchen
to eat dinner instead of eating in my room on a tray. I take
Coco down with me, and she runs up and down to check
on her young, zipped up in their little tent. But on day ten,

when we come back up to the room, I see their bed has been dug up. There are no pups anywhere. For a moment I panic, and I kick myself for all this romanticizing of animals—has she eaten them? But Coco just looks at me sheepishly and crawls under the tent's cushion. There they are, squirming on the cold floor.

I look online—dogs bury their young for warmth, to protect them, but also in preparation for death if they are sick. I text two friends who have had several litters between them. One says it's normal behavior. The other texts back casually, "I'm sure it's nothing but sometimes they do kill their young." I try to stay awake to stand guard, but I fall asleep. Coco wakes me in the dark night, her ears folded back against her head to tell me she's done it again. She buries them four times. I never understand why.

By the second week, two of the puppies have started to crawl out of their tent and onto my pillow. Teeni, the fourth born, is the first to do it, quietly pulling herself along the blanket until she touches my skin. She sleeps between my neck and my face, curled up against me for warmth. Coco pulls her back inside whenever she catches her. Carlo, the last born, whom Allegra has named after an Italian saint, starts to follow his sister. They sleep against me, their puppy breath smelling like forest moss, like stale coffee, wet grass, and rotting tomatoes. Like newborn babies, they try to suckle on my nose and my cheeks when I hold them up to my face. There is nothing secular about this kind of love. It's faith, a blind, burning hope that things will be okay, that something powerful and divine will protect this fragile, delicate life. Because. Because why? I don't know.

My friends think I have been cut off from the world too long. I whisper the *azan* in the puppies' ears one night soon after they are born, echoing Muslim tradition that sings the call to prayer in a newborn's ear after birth so it is the first sound they hear. Only Allegra doesn't think I am crazy, and that's because she blessed them in the name of the Father, Son, and Holy Spirit one day while I was having a shower. "There is a secret language between animals and humans," Allegra says, "tenderness. That's why God gave us animals, so we can watch over each other. They are our guardian angels." I listen to Allegra, who says this with a believer's certainty. She of true faith.

My aunt tells me about research that shows when dogs dream, they dream of their owners. Scientists and veterinary neurologists and others have studied phases of sleep and REM cycles in animals since the 1960s—even Aristotle believed animals dreamed and was certain that dogs barked in their sleep the way we sleep-talk during dream states. We know that rats dream about running around mazes, cats chase and hunt, and zebra finches dream of songs they have learned to sing. I watch the puppies as they fatten and grow, their eyes slowly opening; they start to make noises, growling and hissing in their sleep. What are they dreaming of? I ask my aunt. Probably of drinking milk, she supposes. I wonder if they dream of their mother.

By this point, Coco is relaxing. She is keen to go outside and get away from the puppies, whose nails are starting to scratch her tummy as they headbang during feeding time. She jumps out of their bed now and races downstairs mid-feed, leaving the puppies hanging in limbo, confused, their tongues still searching for teats. That's what mothers do, I want to tell them, they go. They leave.

One morning, I sit with the puppies after Coco has dumped them to go for a hike with Allegra, and I cry, overcome and overwhelmed with everything that has happened this year—the losses, the joys, the failures, this extraordinary act of love and life, the loneliness and worry. They all clamber onto my legs and watch me, heads tilted, newly opened ears standing alert, listening. One of them licks my face. The rest just watch. In some sense, I have been searching for a mother since I was a child. The first time my stepmother called me her stepchild, talking to a friend on the phone, I overheard her and howled. But she was right, I wasn't her child. Time would show that. I think of both of my lost mother figures now and wonder if being childless is my punishment. If I can't have a mother and I cannot be one, then where am I to go? What am I to do with this life of mine?

I hold the puppies and sing to them from the revelation of God. I spend the next month staying awake late at night out of choice, no longer deprivation, so I can watch them and hold the ones that I think will go to other homes, desperate not to lose time. I want to love them without fear. I didn't expect to learn this much about love or God or grace from any of this. I didn't expect to be so moved by the simple act of care.

Chapter 13

That November, I read a story from the pre-pandemic heyday of 2019, about an eerie occurrence in India when 23,000 birds—flamingos, cranes, and others—were found dead on the shores of Rajasthan's Sambhar Lake, India's largest inland salt lake. No one knew what had happened to cause Asia's largest mass fatality of birds. Avian botulism was ruled out at the time; other theories suggested that climate change had caused the lake to dry up and that illegal salt mining further disfigured the birds' natural environment. Could it have been mass starvation? The article I read supposed that it was none of these things but an omen, a harbinger of something terrible to come, a zoonotic plague soon to engulf the world. It was too much to consider and, at the same time, meaningless; meaningless at least for me at that moment, locked down in another sort of plague far away.

Four years later, new research revealed that heavier than normal rainfall that summer had caused salt levels in the lake to drop, which created the perfect conditions for *Clostridium botulinum* to thrive. That fatal bacteria causes avian botulism. Abnormal rainfall and intense monsoon rains now pummel Pakistan and India, by-products of global warming. That is not the only ominous warning to have grown increasingly frightening in the intervening years. Since then, at least twenty-four previously unthinkable heat waves have hit locations across our planet that would have had "zero chance" of occurring without the increasing heat trapped by fossil fuel emissions.[28] It's the burning of fuel, the slashing of our forests, the endless manufacturing; it's unchecked power and violence—in the first 120 days of its air and ground bombardment of Gaza in 2023, Israel released more planet-warming gases into the atmosphere than the annual carbon footprint of the world's twenty most climate-vulnerable nations.[29] Studies looking at the climate emergency's impact on unnatural disasters found that 550 heat waves, floods, wildfires, storms, and droughts had been made "significantly more severe or more frequent by global heating."[30]

You probably remember some of them; maybe you even survived one of them. The biblical flooding in Pakistan that submerged one-third of the country and affected 33 million people; torrential rains in Valencia that saw two months' worth of rainfall in just ten hours; the Los Angeles wildfires that blazed through 58,085 acres; cyclone Chido, which barreled through Mayotte, Mozambique, and Malawi, destroying agricultural land and causing severe food shortages. Will these warnings ever register? I suspect we read these sorts of stories as just more examples of how we have destroyed the world for our short-term comfort. We shake our heads and move on.

The puppies are an endless source of fascination. When they approach Coco with their serrated-knife-like milk teeth, she bolts. I teach them tricks and am enraptured when they seem to have learned their names. Though they are roughly the size of hamsters, they fight like stallions, rearing up on their hind legs to brawl. Everything I own here in Italy is torn and covered in white Jack Russell hair. But my attention has never been so focused on anything quite like this before.

Carlo, the last born, sleeps upside down, hanging off my lap, like a supine bat, head flung back, spotty ears limp. He is only two months old and still seeks flesh and warmth when he sleeps, so he twists and turns, adjusting his floppy body until he finds skin to tuck his nose into. I'm keeping him, the one that bit my lip off not once but several times. Allegra may have named Carlo after a recently beatified saint who died as a young man, but he's more like Carlos the Jackal than Carlo the teenage saint.

Untamed and untrained, the puppies leap at everything, unafraid, ready to best all forces, but except for Carlo, they are equally ready to crouch and lower their ears in submission if defeated. When I put them in their pen to sleep at night, one sticks her head through the bars, another one climbs out of it, and yet another, Carlo, of course, uses his teeth to attempt to unlock the grille. When I scold him, he glares at me and barks. He still doesn't know who is in charge here, me or him. Me, I tell him. I lick their faces and growl at them. I am in charge. But Carlo, with his wild heart, is not convinced by my power.

"For small creatures such as we," Carl Sagan wrote, "the vastness is bearable only through love."[31] It's from his only full work of fiction, the novel *Contact*, about a scientist whose father died when she was a young girl. I think of this line when I am with the pups. They like to sleep on our necks, I later learn, because of the pulse that throbs there, reminding them of their mothers' heartbeat. But touch is also provocative, and I am shredded for my constant forgetting that they are dogs, not babies. I try to show one of them a video and have my bottom lip nearly taken off for my effort. Friends pause when I tell them this. "You were showing the puppies—the puppies?—a video?" "Yes, a video," I say, "it was of a dog watching a horse race. I thought they'd like it."

I know they are not human babies. And though I hunger for motherhood, the thought forming all my waking hours, I don't see how it matters. I see how energy flows, how the puppies are sensitive and receptive to it. The dog you don't gel with is the most aggressive until you pick her up and whisper into the raw shell of her ear. Now she is even-tempered and serene. Over the phone, the man is very supportive of this new fascination of mine. "Yes, yes, dogs are like babies, better than babies, how wonderful." I know he is just manipulating me, it's not even well done at this point, but clunky and desperate. He is also delighted that I am hidden away here in a forest, removed from the real world, and encourages me to stay on for as long as possible. One day, he tells me with what he thinks is wonder in his voice: "You know, you won't believe this, but I feel Coco is like my daughter." He is a fraud. She is *my* companion, *my* Coco, not his daughter or child or anything. She is not even his dog. They are *my* dogs, my beating, barking hearts.

What a terrible thing love is—to be so wholly involved with these lives, from birth through every waking moment of their days, and then to have to let go. You speak into their soft, folded, furry ears and feed them with your fingers and have one bite you, drawing blood, and another one lick your wounds, and then at three months, that's it, they're off to other homes, gone. It is nearly two months when I realize why I know this feeling that has sat with me since they were born, a full and attentive but fearful love. I've had it all my life: the sense that you must love someone with all your might because they will be taken away from you—it's only a matter of time. So, you must love them now and love them strong and hard. I hold the pups when I realize this, utterly overwhelmed.

"If you surrendered to the air, you could ride it," Toni Morrison wrote in *Song of Solomon*, a line that always seemed to me crystalline guidance on how to navigate the terrible anxiety of life.[32] Only the fools among us think they can fight fate and win. But I do not have my father's romance with the world or his radical acceptance of destiny. At times, I am afraid that I will be heartbroken for the rest of my life. I think a lot about broken hearts in my quiet hours of the pandemic. It's a glorious thing, love, for its ability to break and be re-formed, break and be re-formed over and over again. This staying alive is so fragile, so miraculous. Just over two weeks before he was murdered, Malcolm X had been invited to speak to students in Selma, Alabama. Since I first read his autobiography, when I was a teenager, I have been moved by Malcolm X, not just by his fearlessness to speak uncomfortable truths but by his personal journey of struggle and transformation. To me he is a modern prophet of redemption, a seeker and a man whose greatest fight was within himself. In our secluded forest in Italy, in the late hours of the night, sleeping on the floor next to the dogs, I read Malcolm's February 1965 speech from Selma. It's the first time that I've seen this particular address. I read it again and again in the dark, the only light the blue glow of my phone. Later, I find grainy black-and-white video, which I bookmark and listen to on my walks. Standing at the pulpit at the Brown Chapel AME Church, Malcolm X offered a prayer to his people. "I pray that God will bless you and anything that you do," he said, "and I pray that all of the fear that has ever been in your heart will be taken out." This is the greatest benediction one can have—the removal of terror. Only love can bring that.

Chapter 14

Many years ago, I visited Miyajima, a shrine island in Japan known for its population of wild deer. I took a ferry from Hiroshima after a day spent at the museum and walking over the buried ruins of the bombed city. A short boat ride later, we arrived, welcomed by several of the hundreds of the deer that roam freely across the small island. Miyajima's deer are unafraid of people—they approached us casually, sniffing at our pockets and hands. Long ago, the deer were thought to be messengers of the gods. Even Buddha is said to have once lived as a golden deer who sacrificed himself to save a pregnant doe from the King of Benares, hunting in the forests.

I walked through the town, and its market selling sweets and desserts, trailed by the hungry deer. They weren't aggressive, but they were insistent. Where are you going? Who are you? What are you eating? Signs all over warned against feeding the deer, and so I didn't. I took pictures of the floating torii gate, out in the water, of the semi-wild deer tiptoeing through pagodas and manicured gardens. It was otherworldly. The world I know hunts and destroys what it cannot capture and cage. This was something else.

Perhaps more well-known than Miyajima is Nara, home to a park filled with friendly deer as well as Buddhist and Shinto temples. In the years since I visited Japan, pounds of plastic have been found in the dead bodies of Nara's deer. They eat the plastic because it's scented with food—one deer had consumed about ten pounds of plastic. "The deer that died were very skinny," a local vet and conservationist said. "I was able to feel their bones."[33] The more people came to Nara, the more they endangered the deer, officially designated Japanese national treasures in the late 1950s. What does that tell us of our relationship to beauty? We are concerned only by our hunger for it. We are ravenous, and careless. We need beauty to survive this bad world, but we care nothing for how it survives. We feed our garbage to the mystical deer that we travel distances to gawp at. We know we are doing it, but we don't think about anything other than our needs.

In times of grief and anxiety, nature reminds me that there is beauty undisturbed by my pain. It reminds me to be at the mercy of reverence and justice, and it tells me that no matter what happens, the world will carry on without me. The wild—the animals and life outside our orbit and control—was once the only thing true and resilient enough to survive man and the force of our weak, damaged hearts. But soon, in our rapaciousness, we will consume it too.

"I think of beauty as an absolute necessity," Toni Morrison said, "I don't think it's a privilege or indulgence. It's not even a quest. I think it's almost like knowledge, which is to say, it's what we were born for. I think finding and then incorporating beauty is what humans do."[34] From the puppies' birth to when they are biting, barking, running, chewing, three-month-old dogs, my love transfers from one to another to another and back again, blooming, widening, and delighting in something essential that they give me.

I forget that my house is in ruins. I forget that the world is aflame. I forget that the future is a time of uncertainty and that promises of tomorrow are fulfilled to no one. I never forget that I am losing the man, or that he is losing me, but when I am upstairs writing—because they have given me this back too—and the puppies cry for me to come down to them, it sounds like birdsong, soft chirrups. In the loneliness of the pandemic and its lockdowns, they are reminders of joy and the sense that, as Milan Kundera wrote, "Beauty is a rebellion against time."[35]

Chapter 15

The end with the man came slowly, unfolding in several catastrophic parts. The more my eyes opened, the more I questioned all the fantasies I had so readily invented and the cruder the man became in real life. And perceptive as he was, he started to understand what was happening: I no longer respected him. As he sensed this shift in me, he grew meaner, more emboldened, and more unapologetic. He seemed to spool apart before me, in slow motion.

Our final break began with a fight. We were in Granada; he was driving and I was navigating. He was always a pain to give directions to as he so often ignored them, turning right instead of left, asking agitatedly what turn he had to take seconds before having to take it, even though you had told him several times already, and generally having a frustratingly low threshold for error and discovery during road trips. That day, driving through a city neither of us had been to before, he handed me his sunglasses and instructed me to clean them. I could sense his irritation building, so I wiped his sunglasses and handed them back to him in order to focus on the map. "No," he bit out, "they're not clean." I took them, wiped them again, and returned them to him. "No!" the man barked. "Clean them with water."

I knew that if I tried to juggle my phone, his glasses, and a bottle of water, something would go wrong. As calmly as possible, I told him that we had an exit coming up. I spoke as though to a child whose tantrum was gathering. But the man wanted his glasses cleaned now. *How have I made myself captive to this entitled, petulant knobhead?* I thought to myself. And as these thoughts grated at me, in the middle of the highway, the man yanked the bottle of water from the floor.

"Anyone can do two things at once," he hissed. To defend myself by saying I couldn't clean his glasses because I might make a mistake with the navigation would be to humiliate myself further and acknowledge how much I had started to walk on eggshells around him, so I said nothing. His shirt was wet from wiping the glasses, and water had spilled onto his arms and lap. He put his glasses back on and let loose a torrent of insults, not pausing for breath. During the man's rages, I often retreated within myself and tried to block out his cruelties. But that day in the car, I listened to every word he spat at me even as it hurt. My body trembled with a much-delayed rage.

I had Coco and the pups with me, but if I hadn't, I would have opened the car door and walked off. Earlier in the trip, he had thrown a tantrum because I had wondered if the dogs needed to stop for a bathroom break. "Did you even once ask me what I need?" he shouted. "You're a grown man," I reminded him, "they are puppies?" "Did you ask me if I'm thirsty? If I need to stop?" he barreled away with all the indignant misery of a sulking narcissist. On that leg of the drive, a part of me wanted to laugh, it was so ridiculous. Had I wondered if *he* needed a bathroom break? No. Because I was inconsiderate. So, I turned to him and said, in my most concerned voice, "Do you need a bathroom break? Would you like some water? Do you want to stop?" And watched with incredulity as his fury powered down, like a toy running out of battery. My urge to laugh at the absurdity of it all faded. I was sad for what he had done to me and regretful for all the time I had wasted on him. I wanted to be free of the man and this bruising relationship, bereft of kindness and decency. "I'm done," I told him that evening. "I can't go on like this." He didn't want this either, he said. We agreed to end things.

"But just for three months," he hedged. "Let's try it out. With no contact whatsoever. I don't care if you're sick and dying, don't call me, don't text me, I won't answer."

That was fine by me. "Let's start now."

*   *   *

When we parted ways two days later, he texted me from the airport. "Let's not have any contact," I reminded him. "Yes," he agreed. But he texted again when he landed. And the next day. And the day after that. When he tried to call me, I didn't answer. "We have ended things," I reminded him, "no contact for three months." And unlike what I had imagined, all those years ago, would happen when he would threaten to leave me, without the man I was happy. Actually happy. I stopped having debilitating stomachaches; I stopped crying. I went to sleep calmly, and I woke up without interrogatory texts awaiting me. I could do what I liked without fearing a lecture or a barrage of judgment headed my way, and there was no one—no one!—putting me down on a daily basis. I felt liberated, untethered from an insatiable abyss. It was glorious.

Of course, he came back. And he delivered me a new assortment of promises to do with everything I'd ever wanted. Yes, he would have children. Yes, he would get married, yes, yes to whatever I wanted. Though I finally knew him, knew that he would break these oaths just like he had broken all the others, they were the biggest and the most confident of all the vows he had ever sworn to me. I was wary. Not just of his fragile promises but of him. The world is full of men whose hearts are broken and who are unable—untaught or unwilling—to do anything about their pain, the Australian writer Helen Garner noted, and those are the men who become dangerous. But what if it was possible? What if, as he insisted, the man had changed? For about two weeks, he was the nicest I had ever known him to be. He was different, he promised, this time would be different. Even with my suspicions, it was too tempting not to believe him. So I did. It was very short lived.

"When you have a child," the man casually announced over coffee during this time, "you'll have to stop working." "Stop writing?" I couldn't believe what he was saying. The man sipped his quarter shot, mostly milk cappuccino, and confirmed. "Stop writing, stop your talks." "Why?" My face must have been a map of confusion. "You think I'm going to sit there with a baby while you fly off on a book tour to Brazil?" A sliver of disgust passed over the man's eyes, but it passed as he took another sip of his drink. "How will I support myself?" I asked him. "I won't earn anything if I stop working." The man looked down at a muffin he had ordered but hadn't eaten yet, gingerly peeling away the wrapper. "I'll give you money for what you need." I raised my eyebrows. He hadn't even bought the muffin. "*You* will?" I asked. He looked up at me and smiled warmly. "If you're a good wife and you look after me, of course I will."

*   *   *

Once you have seen a beast laid bare, you can never quite unsee it. I am not a wolf by blood, the poet Osip Mandelstam wrote, only my equal can kill me. The man was not my equal. It took me years, but once I saw it, I left him and never, ever looked back.

Chapter 16

have sat with grief too long in my life. But something changed for me in the wake of this loss. I decided that I wouldn't live any longer as a servant of fear and sadness. I learned to let go.

One of the puppies, Stellina, was leaving for her new home. I had come around to her departure and run away from it several times. I knew I couldn't keep six dogs, but why not? "Think of the dogs," friends told me, when it was clear that I was only thinking about myself. "Think of yourself, are you crazy?" other friends shouted. I lost track of who I was supposed to be thinking of, so finally the date was set, the home confirmed. I would give the pups only to people I know, not to strangers—this was the only way I agreed to the breaking up of this small family we had made and loved so briefly and so deeply.

Stellina, who looks so much like Coco, down to the markings on her head and the angel wings on her back, is a biter. She has taken chunks out of my hand, and when she bites, she looks you in the eyes and growls at you with glee, savoring her juicy victory. But she was quiet when I held her on her last days at home, offering her outstretched neck with its little jowls for me to kiss.

The day before she was due to leave, I was in the puppy room and there was a riot. The five of them were agitated and biting, pulling each other's tails, screeching, barking, and taking apart everything I set down, ripping their pee pads in half, chewing the wire netting on their pen, and zooming across the room with sharp objects in their mouths. Over their din, I heard Allegra shouting for me. "Fati," she said, "come quickly—you have to see this—there's deer outside—come and see them!"

I put the biting, barking, squealing puppies in their pen and went outside. "Careful," Allegra said, "you'll scare them away."

The deer were just feet away. I saw two at first, their autumnal brown skin blending into the warm colors of the forest. One had antlers, maybe the other one too, but I couldn't tell through the bare, denuded branches of the winter trees. Allegra whispered that there were four of them. A family. "Coco brought me to them," she said.

Coco was standing, her paws on the glass door, not moving. "She started crying," Allegra continued. I looked at her, confused. "Coco?" Normally Coco would be barking, chasing, running out to yap in the face of any creature that appeared so close to her home. But as we all stood at the door, our breath fogging up the glass, she was soundless, still. I saw them then, the other two deer, as my eyes adjusted to the gloaming and the forest colors. The indigo of the coming night, the earthen yellows and oranges of the leaves, the rich green of the woods. The third and fourth deer were also staring at us, at me, confidently, not lowering their gaze. "I hope it's a good omen," Allegra said.

In Buddhism the deer is the king of the forest, lord of the animals, a meditator in disguise. In Tibetan monasteries, the noble animals flank the dharma wheel, a symbol of Buddhism's teachings, a male and a female golden deer with their ears raised, listening. The pairing is significant, representing harmony, loyalty, happiness. The Hindus associate them with Shiva, the ascetic, the renouncer. In Korean mythology deer are sacred animals, intermediaries between deities and their earthly devotees. The ancient Celts and some Mexican peoples shared this notion of deer as interpreters of the gods, moving between the heavens and the mortal world. Many of the native tribes of North America honored and told stories about these sacred creatures. The Lakota believed deer appeared to lonesome hunters far from home. The Sioux, Cherokee, and Seminole, among others, believed the deer comes as a woman, seducing forlorn men. In Christianity, the deer is depicted as a Christ-like figure.

Saint Eustace, a pagan Roman soldier, was converted after an encounter with a magnificent stag in a moonless forest. He had been hunting when he saw the proud animal with a crucifix held between his antlers. According to the legend, the light of Christ shone out of the deer's eyes, and the voice of God called to Eustace through its lips. Deer are honored in the Psalms, in this Song of David: "He makes my feet like the feet of a deer; he enables me to stand on heights."[36] What would I tell Allegra? That deer have followed me always, that I have a history, a heritage, with these sovereigns of the wild?

The truth is, I thought they had come to say goodbye.

We moved away from the door, even Coco, who remained quiet. I went upstairs to make some phone calls, and Allegra took my place in the room with the pups, letting them continue their rampage, and to say her private farewell to Stellina, whom she had named. Little Star, it means. In my room, from the window I have peered out of a hundred times in search of them, I watched the family of deer in the forest, their white-bottomed tails sparks of light in the near dark. They were still looking at me. They kept their eyes on me. They followed me, turning their heads as I moved to a farther window. Two wandered away into the thicket of trees. But two remained. I think one is the mother, watchful. She is watching over us.

Epilogue

It is three years later, I am forty-one, and now when I leave my flat, I am accompanied by not one Jack Russell terrier but three. For someone who has always tried to live discreetly, I can tell you that bounding about town with a troupe of JRTs is not the way to do so. There is Carlo, the banshee, who waddles out into the street barking wildly to announce to everyone—the neighborhood, fellow dogs, traffic, birds—that he is on the move. He still sleeps upside down, like a floppy-eared bat, and makes sure that all the other dogs in the park know that I am spoken for. Should a dog sniff me or come to be stroked or nuzzled, Carlo stomps over and growls before jumping up to me, making me lift his fat little hind legs, and licking my face, all the while staring at the other dog till they back off. Then there is Tokyo, his older brother, stronger and faster than his stocky sibling, but infinitely more sensitive. He is also part of my protection squad, but his style is slightly different to

Carlo's—less confrontational, more delicate. If he doesn't like the way another dog is getting too friendly with me, he simply lifts his leg and pees on me. Problem solved.

And of course, there is Coco, trying to maintain her distance from her sons so no one will think that she is with them. She's not. She's with *me*. She is nine years old now with wisps of white hair on her brindle snout. At night, while I'm reading, she curls up beside me and looks at me with her big doe eyes. She leans her head against my body while her sons crowd us, Carlo climbing onto the back of the sofa and trying to parachute onto my shoulders and Tokyo sitting on his hind legs and scratching at my arm with his two front paws as he does when he wants to be stroked, which is always. Coco fights her way through the mêlée and gazes at me intently, holding eye contact and seeming to implore me with those wet eyes of hers: Why, she seems to ask, why are these two still here?

Coco appears tired of motherhood, weary of having to chase her errant sons around all day, exhausted from being the household narc who barks madly to alert me every time Carlo steals a sock or stuffs a tissue in his gob, eating it quickly before I can race to the scene and stop him. She mostly ignores Tokyo, acknowledging him only when she wants to steal his food and must snarl at him to do so or if he has caught a ball in the park that she wants. Coco used to be the only dog, top dog, lady of the manor. *La reina,*

Allegra calls her, the queen. She had all the balls, toys, cuddles, and food to herself. And now she has been reduced to part of a pack, a number. One of the dogs, one of the gang, mother of dragons. She is not thrilled about this.

When she has truly had enough and isn't getting the sympathy and outrage from me that she richly deserves, she jumps off the sofa and prances across the room, her nails click-clicking across the floor as she sidles over to Allegra. "Hello, Cocoroni," Allegra murmurs as Coco theatrically flings herself onto her back so Allegra can rub her tummy. She lies at Allegra's feet, her paws bent for the pampering, luxuriating in Allegra's assurance that she's the best of the three. She speaks the best English out of all the dogs and has a fine ear for praise, so she knows very well what is being said. After the belly rub, she jumps up, reclining across Allegra's lap. Before Coco shuts her eyes and drifts to sleep in her auntie's embrace, she looks at me and sighs, her little mouth curling into a smirk.

After the breakup with the man, I had resigned myself to the thought that perhaps the love of Coco and her pups was all the love I would get from life—instead of romance, marriage, and children, I would have the devotion of these creatures, the kindness of my friends, of my community and chosen family.

One winter's night, while taking the dogs for their evening walk, Allegra and I noticed a young priest and two brothers in dark brown robes standing in conversation. Allegra handed me Coco's leash and went to speak to them. They were Dominicans, serving with the Order of the Lamb. I listened to their conversation, keeping my distance, not wanting to intrude even though the dogs pulled me closer, keen to sniff the hems of the brothers' robes. Allegra was earnest and loving and thanked the men for the work they do for the poor while Tokyo jumped up on one of the brothers, inviting him to scratch his head while Coco ignored them and Carlo barked for attention.

Allegra introduced me and said I was her best friend and that these were my dogs, whom she loved. She told the *hermanitos* that she named Carlo after a saint, despite his being the naughtiest of the whole litter. And to my surprise, instead of smiling politely and dismissing us as mad, one of the brothers, *Hermanito* Lucas, asked, "Shall we sing the Franciscan blessing for the animals to them?"

"To them?" I asked. "To the dogs?"

"Yes, the dogs," he replied. "To bless them."

We thanked them, and the men started to sing their hymn. Their voices were so melodious and beautiful that even the three dogs fell silent, sitting back on their hind legs to watch, their little heads cocked. We listened quietly

162

while the brothers finished singing, and in the crisp winter night, for a moment, there was a resonant silence.

Until Carlo barked.

The young priest closed his eyes and said a prayer, blessing the dogs, this family, me and Allegra, asking for us to be safe and happy and protected. I knew I was lucky to have this little family. I bent down and stroked the dogs, one by one, and said *ameen*, the way Muslims pronounce Amen. Carlo's barking continued, echoing against the empty street. "Oh, do shut up Carlo," the *hermanito* with the beautiful voice finally said, as we stood there together with tears in our eyes.

"We do what those who give up the ghost do, we forget our pain," wrote the Palestinian poet Mahmoud Darwish.[37] Though Darwish was not writing about animals, I think of his lines often when reflecting on my life with dogs. With their love, animals remind me that time is elastic and to live well is to remember only that we must live now and do so with purity, free of fear and alive with the possibilities of wonder. I have been lucky to learn so much from dogs. They have taught me about my own failings, forgiven my own lapses of care and kindness, and shown me that it is possible, if you can be true of heart, to redeem those shameful moments.

I still wanted children, very much so. I didn't want to have a child alone, and so I was unsure what to do with the eggs I had frozen. I thought about adopting, imagining that perhaps one day I might, but as selfish as it felt, I had always dreamed of carrying a child, and I was not prepared to abandon that possibility. Some days I told myself that this brood of dogs I lived with was enough. On other days, I knew it was not. On those days I wished, in a way I had never done when I was younger, because I had no idea what I truly wanted then, that maybe, just maybe, if I fell in love with a good man, I might have a chance at the real thing.

Then, it happened. A completely chance encounter as I was out one night at dinner with Allegra. He was sitting at the table next to ours, though mercifully, not close enough to hear our conversation. He was tall and lean, wearing a black sweater and studying a menu. He was American, traveling for work. We started chatting; he seemed friendly and warm. He wanted to know if the food was good at the restaurant; I told him it wasn't. "Did you vote for Trump?" Allegra asked him about two minutes in. "Do you like dogs?" I interrupted. (He didn't. And he does.) After his brief interrogation, Allegra excused herself to go back to the dogs, who needed walking (they didn't), and he asked if I knew a better restaurant nearby (I did).

At that first dinner, he told me about the book he was reading, a collection of stories by Kurt Vonnegut. I told him

I was a writer, and when he got back to his hotel that evening, he texted me and asked if I'd share with him something I'd written. Without thinking, I chose an excerpt of this very book—written as a stand-alone piece years before and published by *Granta*. It was about Coco and her first pregnancy. It felt, in that moment, important for him to read. I tried not to take it personally when, the next morning, he texted back the one word every writer dreads: "Interesting."

Before he returned home to New Jersey, he bought me a copy of the Vonnegut stories and tucked a sweet note for me inside one of the other books on my shelf to find later. He had always wanted children, made me playlists of music he thought I'd like, and sent me pictures of things he had seen while cycling. Once, early on, I missed a message he had sent me—a video he had taken out in a forest. I apologized and explained that I was stuck on a work call but would watch his video immediately after. "Please don't ever feel compelled to respond immediately," he texted back. "I will never take it personally if you don't answer in a day or week or month. It's the only way this can work." He was gentle and sweet but also mature. As I wondered what to text back to express how refreshing he was, how communicative and unusual, he sent another message. "Also, please get back to me if it has been a month."

We spent time getting to know each other, but I didn't want to have another long-distance relationship, I told him. He had never had one before, he confessed, a detail that reassured me greatly. And so we didn't have one. He moved so we were no longer apart, and we got married in my grandfather's library in my family home in Karachi.

Together, we have formed the family I always wanted. Besides being kind, he is intelligent, hardworking, and considerate—and funny, though I didn't think so when he gifted me a book entitled *Jack Russell Training Manual* for Valentine's Day. As it turned out, he was being completely serious and has brought some much-needed discipline and order to this band of rogues. The dogs lavish attention on him, enjoying his assimilation into our pack. Coco flirts with him, staring at me victoriously whenever she gets a belly rub, and makes sure to be the first one to jump up onto the sofa so she can beat the boys and sleep beside him as he reads. Carlo steals his socks, because even though it's been long enough that he knows he should hide them, he still forgets and leaves them in his shoes. Tokyo delights in doing sporty things with him, catching balls and Frisbees and running fast. As he matures as an athlete, Tokyo is less nervous and now understands the rules of bringing things back and waiting politely till they are flung out into space for him to retrieve again. He also pees on me less often.

And me, I am happy. As I write this, I am pregnant, nearly five months along. I can feel my baby kick now; after weeks of asking my obstetrician what kicks feel like ("You'll know when it happens, Fatima"), I finally got my answer: like a ripple moving tight against your skin. It reminds me of the feeling you get in your belly just before you laugh. Every time the baby kicks, I stop what I am doing and watch. It's extraordinary. It's all I ever dreamed of. Many have said that the only way to go through life is without expectation. To live without certainty and love people as they need to be loved, without wanting anything in return, without anticipation or worry. "And I am out on a limb," one of my favorite poets, Frank O'Hara, wrote, "and it is the arm of God."[38]

This, for me, has been a liberation. To learn, very belatedly, that love can and must uplift you and illuminate you instead of oppressing and wounding you has been a joyous discovery. More than joyous, it has been transformative, it has been radicalizing. I'm writing again, my husband finds week-by-week pregnancy videos for us to watch on YouTube, and the dogs are always there, by our side, Carlo sleeping on my belly, as we make our way through the daily victories and defeats of ordinary life, taking every day as it comes: as a blessing.

Acknowledgments

My abiding and eternal gratitude to Allegra, who has been family, friend, refuge, and consigliere to me since the day I met her. She always insists that guardian angels exist and promises me that I have one. I know I do, it's her. Pankaj Mishra has seen me through so much writing and reading in my life, but more than that, he has been a true friend in dark and quiet moments. I'm truly grateful to have a friend like him. My life would have been unbearably lonely without my brother Zulfikar Ali Bhutto. I thank him for his protection and love. Carl Bromley saw this book in several forms and pointed me toward the Bergman film early on in its writing. He has always been a great champion of the underbaked work I show him. Thank you to Marie-Christine de Laubarède for her friendship and shelter at Lime Close in those strange months of the pandemic. Friends read parts of this book when it was not yet a book exactly, but an essay or fragments of what would become a book, and others offered advice when I was stuck without me quite explaining what I was working on. Thank you to Max Porter, David Davidar, John Freeman, Lisa Lucas, and dearest Dustin Schell. Even more friends helped me along, without whom I would have been truly lost. My heartfelt thanks to Sophie Hackford, Ortensia Visconti, Cyril de Commarque, and Cyrus Habib.

Thank you to Sigrid Rausing for giving an early version of this story a home in *Granta*. My agents, Binky Urban and Karolina Sutton, offered all the right advice at the right moments—insisting that something was missing when it was just a book about a dog—and reacting swiftly when it became what it is now. I'm so grateful for their guidance, and to Binky for calling me while I was on the tube one day and telling me she had someone I *had* to talk to and who was going to call me in fifteen minutes. I've been lucky to work with wonderful editors during my life as a writer, but Katie Raissian, whose energy and notes were inspiring and energizing from day one, has been a true gift. I would not have been able to transform this book without her and relied on her to take me through shaky moments. I'm indebted to Marigold Atkey in very much the same way and can't remember enjoying the editing process quite as much as I have working with these two phenomenal editors. Thank you to Marigold for her keen eye and incisive questions. And to Joie Asuquo for her editorial notes and

Susan M. S. Brown for her copyedits. Thank you to Shani Hinton for advice, as always.

I'd be remiss not to thank Dr. Stefano de Guttry, the best vet in the world. And not to mention some of the shelters that do God's work taking in and caring for abused and abandoned dogs. If you're looking for a place to donate, please consider the following:

PAKISTAN: ACF Animal Rescue, LAPS, CDRS Benji
LEBANON: Rescuing in Lebanon, Doggos in Leb, Beta
   Lebanon
GAZA: Sulala Animal Rescue*

Last, this would be a very different book and I would be a very different person had I not had the extraordinary fortune of meeting Graham Byra. Thank you, Graham, for restoring my faith and showing me what it means to love without fear, for all the nights when you did the night feeds so I could wake up and write, for looking after our nutty, glorious dogs, which you mostly seem to enjoy. I thank you with all my heart for making me a mother—the only thing I have ever wanted in life—for being such a warm, present, and joyous father, and for promising me that we can adopt a fourth dog.

* acfanimalrescue.org, lapsglobal.org, cdrsbenji.org, rescuinginlebanon.com, doggosinleb.wordpress.com, betalebanon.org, sulala.ps. They are all on Instagram as well.

Sources

Chapter 1

1 Barry Lopez, *Of Wolves and Men* (New York: Scribner, 1979), loc. 1285, 1293.
2 Friedrich Nietzsche, *Ecce Homo* (New York: Dover Publications, 2004), p. 54.

Chapter 2

3 https://www.bbc.co.uk/religion/religions/buddhism/beliefs/four nobletruths_1.shtml and Damien Keown, *A Dictionary of Buddhism* (Oxford: Oxford University Press, 2004), p. 96.

Chapter 3

4 Frans de Waal, *Mama's Last Hug: Animal Emotions and What They Tell Us About Ourselves* (New York: W. W. Norton, 2019), p. 48.

Chapter 4

5 John Bradshaw, *In Defence of Dogs* (London: Penguin Books, 2012), p. 3.

Sources

6 Alexandra Horowitz, *Inside of a Dog: What Dogs See, Smell, and Know* (New York: Scribner, 2009), p. 39.

7 Bradshaw, p. 4.

8 Bradshaw, p. 69.

9 Bradshaw, p. 51.

10 Horowitz, p. 41.

11 Bradshaw, p. 49.

12 Bradshaw, p. 50.

13 Bradshaw, p. 37.

14 Horowitz, p. 46.

15 https://www.theguardian.com/science/2022/aug/22/dogs-produce-tears-when-reunited-with-owners-study-finds.

16 https://www.theguardian.com/science/article/2024/sep/04/dogs-remember-names-toys-years-study-pets-memory.

17 https://www.theguardian.com/science/2024/mar/22/dogs-understand-meaning-nouns-research-finds.

18 https://www.theguardian.com/lifeandstyle/2022/jan/17/dog-cognition-science.

19 https://www.dawn.com/news/1600383.

20 Bertolt Brecht, "To Those Born After," Edited by John Willett in *Bad Time for Poetry* (London: Methuen, 1995).

Chapter 6

21 Marcel Proust, *Remembrance of Things Past, Within a Budding Grove*, translated by C. K. Scott Moncrieff, D. J. Enright (Vintage Classics, 1996), p. 214.

Chapter 7

22 Koran 27:88. https://quran.com/en/an-naml/88.

Sources

Chapter 10

23 Omar Sakr, "Diary of a Non-Essential Worker," in *Non-Essential Work* (Brisbane: University of Queensland Press, 2024), p. 57.

Chapter 11

24 https://www.newyorker.com/magazine/2018/03/12/when-twenty-six -thousand-stinkbugs-invade-your-home.
25 "When Twenty-Six Thousand Stinkbugs Invade."
26 Rudyard Kipling, *The Second Jungle Book* (Auckland: Floating Press, 2010), p. 30.

Chapter 12

27 Frank Gado, *The Passion of Ingmar Bergman* (Durham: Duke University Press, 1986), p. 349.

Chapter 13

28 https://www.theguardian.com/environment/2024/nov/18/ climate-crisis-to-blame-for-dozens-of-impossible-heatwaves-studies -reveal.
29 https://www.theguardian.com/world/article/2024/jun/06/rebuilding -gaza-climate-cost.
30 https://www.theguardian.com/environment/2024/nov/18/ climate-crisis-to-blame-for-dozens-of-impossible-heatwaves-studies -reveal.
31 Carl Sagan, *Contact* (New York: Simon & Schuster, 1985), p. 94.
32 Toni Morrison, *Song of Solomon* (New York: Knopf, 1995), p. 363.

Sources

Chapter 14

33 https://www.theguardian.com/world/2019/jul/10/japans-famous-nara
-deer-dying-from-eating-plastic-bags#:~:text=Rie%20Maruko%2C%20
a%20vet%20and,bones%2C"%20Maruko%20told%20Kyodo.

34 Toni Morrison, "The Art of Fiction" No. 134 (Fall 1993), interview by
Elissa Schappell and Claudia Brodsky Lacour, *Paris Review,* in recording
but not print edition (online archive *Paris Review,* at theparisreview.org;
accessed June 22, 2020).

35 Milan Kundera, *The Book of Laughter and Forgetting*, translated by Aaron
Asher (New York: HarperCollins, 1994), p. 73.

Chapter 16

36 Bible 2 Samuel 22:34 (New International Version).

Epilogue

37 Mahmoud Darwish, "State of Siege," translated by Ramsis Amun, tran-
scribed by Zdravko Saveski, https://www.arabicnadwah.com/arabic
poetry/darwish-siege.htm#google_vignette.

38 https://www.nytimes.com/2022/06/22/magazine/frank-ohara-poet
.html.